Understanding Bourdieu

Understanding Bourdieu

Jen Webb, Tony Schirato
and Geoff Danaher

SAGE Publications
London ● Thousand Oaks ● New Delhi

First published in 2002 by
Allen & Unwin
83 Alexander Street
Crows Nest NSW 2065
Australia

© Jen Webb, Tony Schirato and Geoff Danaher, 2002
Reprinted 2004, 2005

SAGE Publications Ltd
1 Oliver's Yard, 55 City Road
London EC1Y 1SP

SAGE Publications Inc
2455 Teller Road
Thousand Oaks, California 91320

SAGE Publications India Pvt Ltd
B-42 Panchsheel Enclave
Post Box 4109
New Delhi 100 017

British Library Cataloguing in Publication data

A catalogue record for this book is available from the
British Library

0 7619 7462 8 (hbk)
0 7619 7463 6 (pbk)

Set in 10.5/13pt Palatino by Midland Typesetters
Printed and bound in Great Britain by
Athenaeum Press Ltd., Gateshead, Tyne & Wear

Contents

Acknowledgements

The authors gratefully acknowledge the following for permission to reproduce material in this book: Blackwell Publishers/Polity Press, Cambridge, UK, and the University of Chicago Press, Chicago, for excerpts from *An Invitation to Reflexive Sociology*, by Pierre Bourdieu and Loïc J.D. Wacquant (1992).

We also offer heartfelt thanks to our editors, Elizabeth Weiss and Emma Cotter, for their continual encouragement and patience (and occasional discipline), and the meticulous care they take over our words.

And, finally, our thanks to Professor Bourdieu, who has given us so much to think on, and whose social passion continues to inspire us.

1

Glossary

agency—The idea that individuals are equipped with the ability to understand and control their own actions, regardless of the circumstances of their lives: usually termed 'intentionality' and 'individuality'. We exercise agency, for example, when we indicate our intention to vote one way or another, or make choices about what to eat from a restaurant menu. For Bourdieu, the possibilities of agency must be understood and contextualised in terms of their relation to the objective structures of a culture.

alienation—The concept of alienation comes from Marx, and refers to the estrangement of humanity from nature. In a more specific sense, it refers to the situation where social activities and institutions are commoditised and dominated by the power and logic of the market. Sports such as football have been alienated from people's tribal loyalties and made into a business (see 'commoditisation').

autonomous pole—That part of a field that tends to operate according to principles derived from the field itself and which tends therefore to be isolated and removed from the rest of society. An autonomous principle of the artistic field, for example, is the belief in 'art for art's sake' (See also 'heteronomous pole').

bodily hexis—The physical attitudes and dispositions which emerge in individuals as a result of the relationships between particular fields and individuals' habitus. The bodily hexis of someone from the artistic field, for example, might be expressed through flamboyant gestures and unconventional dress sense.

bureaucrats/bureaucracy—For Bourdieu, bureaucrats make up a 'state nobility' who act as intermediaries between the community and the government, implementing the government's policies, and providing the public with a voice in government.

commoditisation—The term refers to the process of producing or considering something predominantly in terms of its exchangeability.

consecration—The way in which certain positions or practices within a field become endowed with a special aura and sense of distinction denied other practices. The figure of the musical or artistic genius, for example, is a form of consecration.

construction—The notion that objects of research exist for researchers only within the framework of their hypothesis. For Bourdieu, the fundamental scientific act is the construction of the object of research.

cultural arbitrary—A term Bourdieu uses to suggest that the differential power relations pertaining to our culture have no necessary basis but are rather arbitrarily constructed to reflect the interests of dominant groups.

cultural capital—A form of value associated with culturally authorised tastes, consumption patterns, attributes, skills and awards. Within the field of education, for example, an academic degree constitutes cultural capital.

cultural field—Bourdieu's metaphor for representing sites of cultural practice. A cultural field can be defined as a series of institutions, rules, rituals, conventions, categories, designations and appointments which constitutes an objective hierarchy, and which produce and authorise certain discourses and activities. But a field is also constituted by, or out of, the conflict which is involved when groups or individuals attempt to determine what constitutes capital within that field and how that capital is to be distributed.

cultural literacy—A strategic engagement with the field based upon self-reflexivity, an understanding of the rules, regulations and values of the field, and an ability to negotiate conditions and contexts moment by moment.

cultural trajectories—The movement across and between various fields that constitutes an individual's history and which therefore shapes their habitus.

discourse—The forms of language associated with, and expressing the values of, particular cultural fields. A legal discourse, for example, expresses the values and beliefs of the field of law.

disinterestedness—The appearance of being above and removed from areas of economic and social interest. For example, certain artists disavow an interest in being commercial, claiming to be concerned only with 'higher' aesthetic values.

distinction—A kind of habitus, or set of acquired tastes, that is associated with the upper classes, but which has become more generally naturalised as good and noble. A taste for fine wine, classical music and great works of art are examples of markers of distinction.

doxa—A set of core values and discourses which a field articulates as its fundamental principles and which tend to be viewed as inherently true and necessary. For Bourdieu, the 'doxic attitude' means bodily and unconscious submission to conditions that are in fact quite arbitrary and contingent.

empiricism—The study of social phenomena and sense experience, based on systems of measurement rather than on argument alone. For Bourdieu, empiricism is only scientific if its theoretical principles are clearly understood and well thought out, that is, reflexive.

ethnology—A social science related to anthropology, in which the researcher observes the 'natives' or indigenous populations.

epistemology—A concept related to theories about knowledge. Bourdieu calls on sociologists to practise 'epistemological vigilance', reflecting on their own social contexts and conditions, ways of thinking and prejudices that colour their view of the world.

field of power—Bourdieu's metaphor for the ways in which cultural fields actually conduct themselves. 'Power' operates as a meta-field or macro-concept to describe the way in which individuals and institutions in dominant fields (such as government, the law and business) relate to one another and the whole social field. The field of power operates as a configuration of capital (economic, cultural and symbolic) that shapes relations and practices within these fields.

genealogy—A Nietzschean term used to outline an approach that engages with the way in which values, discourses, traditions and rituals that characterise a field, and which present themselves as common sense and permanent, have been historically constructed.

globalisation—The cultural, social and economic movement that displaces people, goods and values from local or national settings and makes them subject to global forces.

habitus—A concept that expresses, on the one hand, the way in which individuals 'become themselves'—develop attitudes and dispositions—and, on the other hand, the ways in which those individuals engage in practices. An artistic habitus, for example, disposes the individual artist to certain activities and perspectives that express the culturally and historically constituted values of the artistic field.

heterodoxy—The set of beliefs and values that challenge the status quo and received wisdom—or common sense—within a particular field. For example, Bourdieu refers to artists as heterodoxical because of the freedom they claim from social norms (see also 'orthodoxy').

heteronomous pole—That part of a field bound up in relations with other fields and expressing their values. The impact of economic values and business imperatives on the field of education, for example, is an expression of heteronomous forces (see also 'autonomous pole').

illusio—The fact of being caught up in and by the game, of believing that the game is worth playing and recognising its stakes. A politician, for example, will demonstrate illusio by believing that the political field constitutes the 'only game in town'.

inalienable values—These are values that are held to be intrinsic to the person and therefore not subject to the values of the market. Inalienable values include honour, loyalty and family allegiance.

instrumental positivism—The paradigm (or set of theoretical principles) that Bourdieu sees as having informed social research and analysis in the United States, in which quantitative research data is used by psychologists, criminologists and sociologists as an instrument for 'knowing' and regulating populations.

intellectualism/intellectual bias—The tendency for certain agents within fields such as the arts and academia to abstract practices as ideas for contemplation rather than problems to be solved. It can lead researchers to take up research problems principally because they are academically interesting, not 'real' social problems.

metaliteracy—The capacity to move across different perspectives and different ways of seeing and appearing. An agent who exhibits metaliteracy will be able to identify the range of different perspectives people hold on a specific issue based on their position within particular fields and social contexts, and will therefore be able to discuss the issue in ways that make sense to these people.

misrecognition—The form of forgetting that social agents are caught up in and produced by. When we feel comfortable within our roles within the social world, they seem to us like second nature and we forget how we have actually been produced as particular kinds of people.

objectivism—The idea that people's actions and attitudes are determined by objective social structures such as those relating to class, ethnicity, gender and language. For example, whether you come from an upper or lower social class will determine your beliefs and behaviour (see also 'subjectivism').

orthodoxy—Those sets of beliefs and values that constitute the received wisdom and the status quo within a field. The orthodoxy reflects the 'official history' of the field: that version of events preserved in official records and documents, authoritative publications and practices (see also 'heterodoxy').

practical sense—An ability to understand and negotiate positions within cultural fields, comparable to a sportsperson's 'feel' for the game.

radical and hyperbolic doubt—The consistent disposition to doubt and question the received wisdom, values and logic that a field presents as its common sense, along with the claims that fields make on behalf of themselves. Bourdieu writes that we 'can never doubt too much'.

reflexivity—Bourdieu asks researchers to adopt a reflexive attitude towards our practices, reflecting upon how forces such as social and cultural background, our position within particular fields and intellectual bias shape the way we view the world.

reproduction—The tendencies of fields such as education to reproduce existing social inequalities rather than challenging or transforming the status quo.

ressentiment—A Nietzschean term, referring to the transformation of a dominated or exploited state or condition into something positive or valuable.

scholastic disposition—The particular perspective on the world held by those within scholarly fields, which can lead to an intellectualising of social issues and problems.

scholastic point of view—The objectifying and universalising perspective offered by a position within the academy.

skholé—The particular kind of 'free time' for scholarly contemplation that Bourdieu sees as the condition of existence of all scholarly fields.

structuralism—A body of theory and system of analysis which informs practices in academic fields such as linguistics, anthropology, cultural studies, Marxism and psychoanalysis. Structuralism is basically the view that the social world is organised according to structures—rules, systems and forms—and that these make meaning possible.

subjectivism—A perspective asserting that social reality is produced through the thoughts, decisions and actions of individual agents. The conventional Hollywood hero, for example, embodies the subjectivist perspective in the way in which he shapes reality through his decisions and actions (see also 'objectivism').

symbolic capital—A form of capital or value that is not recognised as such. Prestige and a glowing reputation, for example, operate as symbolic capital because they mean nothing in themselves, but depend on people believing that someone possesses these qualities.

symbolic violence—The violence which is exercised upon individuals in a symbolic, rather than a physical way. It may take the form of people being denied resources, treated as inferior or being limited in terms of realistic aspirations. Gender relations, for example, have tended to be constituted out of symbolic violence which has denied women the rights and opportunities available to men.

universalise—To treat a set of values derived from a particular field as though they are universally applicable across every field. For instance, academics may attempt to universalise the value of contemplative reflection and regard it as a form of behaviour to which everyone should aspire.

validation and discovery—These are the two distinct logics applied in sociology. The belief tends to be that the discovery moment is relegated to the world of chance or the 'non-rational', while validation is regarded as genuinely 'scientific'. For Bourdieu, discovery is every bit as 'scientific' as validation, because it is the basis of speculation leading to constructing a hypothesis and then a research program.

1

Contexts and approaches

As well as being, in the words of Richard Shusterman, 'France's leading living social theorist' (Shusterman 1999: 1), Pierre Bourdieu is, along with Michel Foucault and Jacques Derrida, one of the most influential of those French thinkers 'whose work succeeded structuralism' (Calhoun et al. 1993: 7). There are few aspects of contemporary cultural theory (which crosses fields such as cultural studies, literary studies, anthropology, sociology, philosophy, gender studies, psychoanalysis and film and media studies) to which Bourdieu has not made a significant contribution. His concepts of habitus, field and capital, for instance, constitute what is arguably the most significant and successful attempt to make sense of the relationship between objective social structures (institutions, discourses, fields, ideologies) and everyday practices (what people do, and why they do it). Most of the 'big' theoretical issues being debated and explored in the world of contemporary theory—gender and subjectivity, the 'production' of the body, communicative ethics, the public sphere and citizenship, the politics of cultural literacy, the relationship between capitalism, culture and cultural consumption, 'ways of seeing', the transformation of society through the forces of globalisation—are to some extent explicable in terms of, and have benefited from, Bourdieu's 'technologies' of habitus, field and capital.

And yet, 30 years after his books started becoming widely available in English translation, Bourdieu's status is far more peripheral than that of Foucault, with whom he shares so many theoretical interests and inclinations; and his work 'continues to befuddle many of his Anglo-American readers' (Wacquant in Calhoun et al. 1993: 237). Loïc Wacquant has put forward a number of explanations for this phenomenon, ranging from the inability of critics to categorise satisfactorily Bourdieu's body of work, to the 'vociferous indignation' (1993: 237) that has sometimes greeted his writing style.

The second explanation does not really hold water: as Wacquant himself writes, other 'difficult' writers such as Foucault and Habermas 'do not elicit the same level of protestation as the author of *Distinction*' (1993: 247). The first explanation, however, requires more attention. Calhoun et al. have noted that 'In a series of research projects and publications starting in the 1950s, Bourdieu has addressed an astonishing range of empirical topics and theoretical themes' in areas such as 'education, labor, kinship, economic change, language, philosophy, literature, photography, museums, universities, law, religion, and science' (1993: 1). One of the consequences of this eclecticism is that unlike, say, Foucault, there is no clear sense of theoretical 'progression', no easily identifiable 'stages' or paths, to Bourdieu's career.

Bourdieu's eclecticism

The narrative of Bourdieu's theoretical and disciplinary interests and affiliations is certainly peripatetic. He started out as a philosopher influenced by the work of Martin Heidegger and the phenomenologist Maurice Merleau-Ponty, but his interest in Algeria saw him forego philosophy for anthropology, which was then very much under the influence of structuralists such as Claude Lévi-Strauss. However, his dissatisfaction with the inability of structuralist anthropology to take into account or make sense of the practical (and strategic) dimensions of everyday life led to two of his most famous critiques of anthropology, *Outline of a Theory of Practice* (1977a) and *The Logic of Practice* (1990b).

Bourdieu also turned his attention to two other areas of study: education and culture. His works on education focused on the role that secondary and tertiary education play in reproducing social and cultural classification and stratification; the 'education' books that have attracted most attention in the English-speaking world include *Reproduction in Education, Society and Culture* (1977b) and *Homo Academicus* (1988). Perhaps the best known of his books in English, *Distinction: A Social Critique of the Judgement of Taste* (1984), is an empirically based critique of Kantian aesthetics. More recently, Bourdieu has extended his interest in the field of cultural production by writing the strongly polemical *On Television* (1998c); and this more openly 'interventionist' approach has also resulted in books on the politicising of arts funding (*Free Exchange* (1995), with the German artist Hans Haacke), gender relations, in *Masculine Domination* (2001), the everyday pressures and predicaments of lower class groups in contemporary France in the multi-authored *The Weight of the World* (1999a) and globalisation and the withdrawal of the state from social life, in *Acts of Resistance: against the New Myths of our Time* (1998b). Finally, he has recently written three books—*Practical Reason: on the Theory of Action* (1998d), *Pascalian Meditations* (2000) and *Masculine Domination* (2001)—which clarify and elaborate upon, in a quite personal way, his work, methodologies, theories and relations to different fields such as philosophy, history and sociology.

Bourdieu can be categorised as a social scientist, but his work, in Loïc Wacquant's words:

> throws a manifold challenge at the current divisions and accepted modes of thinking of social science by virtue of its utter disregard for disciplinary boundaries, the unusually broad spectrum of domains of specialized inquiry it traverses . . . and its ability to blend a variety of sociological styles, from painstaking ethnographic accounts to statistical models, to abstract metatheoretical and philosophical arguments. (1992d: 3)

Bourdieu not only consistently makes use of both empirical and theoretical methodologies; he considers them inseparable. This has tended to set his work apart from much of the Anglo-American social sciences, which tend to be positivist and largely eschew theory; and the more philosophically-oriented fields (philosophy, literature, cultural studies), which are highly suspicious, if not downright disdainful, of empirical methodologies.

Throughout his academic career Bourdieu has usually found himself writing as a sociologist 'in someone else's field'; or at least writing on topics (education, art, philosophy, literature, language) that are claimed as the domain of specific fields, and are largely understood in terms of the discourses, debates, traditions, theories, methodologies and imperatives of those fields.

This eclecticism provides Bourdieu's work with two distinctive virtues. The first is that as a 'visiting' non-specialist, he is relatively free to move across fields such as art history or linguistics without being directed by the 'ways of seeing' of that field. And, as a corollary, he is also free both to ignore issues or problems which practitioners might consider essential to their thinking or enquiries, and to ask questions, or pursue lines of enquiry, which might be unthinkable to those closely involved with the field and its ways of thinking.

The second advantage Bourdieu takes from his eclecticism is that he is able to use insights derived from different theorists to transform bodies of knowledge and give them a practical—that is to say, political—'edge', or dimension. The best example of this is probably his extension of the sociolinguist J.L. Austin's work on speech act theory. Austin does a great deal to describe and analyse the conventions that inform practices of speaking but, more or less typically of his field, he pays very little attention to the institutional contexts that produce, govern and direct those conventions. In *Language and Symbolic Power* (1991a), Bourdieu builds on Austin's work in order to investigate how speech act conventions are naturalised, and which groups benefit from them.

The politicising of theory

An example of the difference between the two approaches can be seen if we look at what is involved when a judge declares, say, that a group of people are guilty of terrorism. For Austin, what is important are the details (certain court rituals and procedures, the sort of language used, the judge's title and robes, the arrangement of furniture in the courtroom) which determine whether the act is 'felicitous' (in other words, that it is a real judge in a real court, and the words 'I find you guilty of terrorism' have real consequences), or 'infelicitous' (that is, it is just someone acting out a part, and the consequences of the words cannot be enforced).

For Bourdieu, on the other hand, there are other, more important issues that need to be followed up, such as the fact that a representative of the government, the legal system and the upper classes is in a position to evaluate certain behaviour (say, opposition to the government, the legal system and the upper classes) as 'terrorism', and to treat the 'terrorists' accordingly. Terrorism is not an unequivocal or unchanging state, regardless of what 'legitimate authorities' say. There is a joke in the British comedy series *Yes Minister* where Sir Humphrey points out that one thing that many of the great world leaders have in common is that they were all imprisoned, at one time, by the British. Nelson Mandela is another example of this process: he was convicted (by legitimate institutions) of terrorism, but his activities are now understood as a struggle for freedom.

Marx, Wittgenstein, Nietzsche and Pascal

This development of Austin's speech act theory is quite typical of Bourdieu's work. Austin's formalist analysis is 'taken somewhere else' by Bourdieu—in short, it is politicised. In this section we will provide a brief, introductory description of the theories and approaches—pre-eminently taken from Friedrich Nietzsche, Karl Marx, Blaise Pascal and Ludwig Wittgenstein—which we argue have provided Bourdieu with this 'politicising disposition'.

We pointed out that Bourdieu is one of the most eclectic of contemporary cultural theorists, drawing on important scholars from a number of historical periods and geographical locations, and from various academic disciplines. As well as his obvious links with, and debts to, sociologists such as Emile Durkheim, Max Weber, Norbert Elias and Marcel Mauss, Bourdieu also borrows from, and crosses into, other fields—so much so that his bibliographies read like libraries in themselves. He draws, for instance, from anthropology (Clifford Geertz, Claude Lévi-Strauss), art history (Erwin Panofsky), the history of science (Gaston Bachelard, Georges Canguilhem), linguistics (J.L. Austin, Emile Benveniste), phenomenology (Edmund Husserl, Maurice Merleau-Ponty), philosophy (Martin Heidegger, Immanuel Kant), political economy (M. Polanyi), psychology (Sigmund Freud) and social anthropology (Harold Garfinkle, Erving Goffman). All these influences have, at different times, 'surfaced' in Bourdieu's writing, but the four theorists we referred to above 'stand behind' and inform both the content of his work and, even more importantly, his purposes in producing it.

While there is widespread acceptance of the importance of Marx, Wittgenstein and Pascal to Bourdieu's work, the same is not true of the nineteenth-century German philosopher, Friedrich Nietzsche. He is usually considered less influential than the sociologists Durkheim, Weber and Mauss, the philosopher Heidegger, or the phenomenologist Merleau-Ponty. Books about Bourdieu's work and theories (such as Harker, Mahar & Wilkes 1990; Calhoun et al. 1993; or Shusterman 1999), allocate considerable space, for instance, to Bourdieu's relation to Marx, but rarely mention Nietzsche.

To a certain extent, Bourdieu has contributed to this impression: in the various collections of essays and interviews where he discusses his theoretical influences most openly (such as *In Other Words, Sociology in Question, An Invitation to Reflexive Sociology* and *Practical Reason*) he rarely enters into any detailed discussion or analysis of Nietzsche's work, usually confining himself to a combination of brief dismissals or qualifications of his worth, or quoting from, or referring to, him in an understated way.

An Invitation to Reflexive Sociology typifies this—it contains only five references to Nietzsche. One reference is in a section of the book written by Loïc Wacquant, and distances Bourdieu from any significant relation to Nietzsche. Wacquant writes, 'His is not a Nietzschean vision of "a universe of absolute functionality"' (1992d: 52). Bourdieu himself only refers to Nietzsche on two occasions in the book: once to 'put him in his place', writing (disapprovingly) of 'the exaltation of the works of Nietzsche or Heidegger' which 'leads to an *aestheticism* of transgression' (1992d: 154); and once to invoke him, fleetingly, as an authority with regard to a definition of the concept of *ressentiment*—that is, what Bourdieu refers to as 'the sentiment of the person who transforms a sociologically mutilated being . . . into a model of human excellence . . . built upon an unconscious fascination with the dominant' (1992d: 212). And this in a book which is heavily indebted to the Nietzschean notion of ressentiment.

The example he gives of ressentiment, appropriately enough, is concerned with the need to question why a person is writing from, or taking, a particular position, as when Bourdieu asks of himself, 'Isn't the root of my revolt . . . of the rhetorical vibration of my adjectives when I describe Giscard d'Estaing playing tennis . . . the fact that, deep down, I envy what he is?' (1992d: 212). That he extrapolates from the notion of ressentiment in order to negotiate and rethink the imperatives and values of the field of sociology clearly demonstrates the importance of Nietzsche to Bourdieu's thinking—but it is an importance which is almost deliberately covered over by Bourdieu, and his associates such as Loïc Wacquant. This 'overlooking' of Nietzsche is in contrast to the very central role accorded to Marx, Wittgenstein and Pascal by commentators, particularly with regard to Bourdieu's borrowing and reworking of the Marxist concepts of capital and class; Pascal's emphasis on the relation between bodily rituals and the inculcation of belief; and Wittgenstein's questioning of the 'intellectualising' of practical experience.

Marx and Wittgenstein

What are the main insights and approaches that Bourdieu takes from these four theorists? Let us consider Marx and Wittgenstein first. We pointed out earlier that one of Bourdieu's main virtues as a theorist is his ability to take bodies of theory and give them a 'practical' or political edge. He more or less refuses the idea of writing or theorising as a form of 'disinterested reflection'—a position traditionally associated with philosophy. Rather, he sees his scholarly work as a means to an end—as changing or 'doing' things.

To a large extent this is something that Bourdieu takes from both Marx and Wittgenstein. Bourdieu ends the strongly person-alised first chapter of *Pascalian Meditations* with the following quote—inserted more or less as a coda for the rest of the book—from Wittgenstein:

> What is the use of studying philosophy if all that it does for you is to enable you to talk with some plausibility about some abstruse questions of logic . . . and if it does not improve your thinking about the important questions of everyday life, if it does not make you more conscientious than any . . . journalist in the use of the *dangerous* phrases such people use for their own ends? (Wittgenstein quoted in Bourdieu 2000: 42)

In his discussion of Bourdieu's reading and use of Austin's work, James Bohman describes Bourdieu as 'a constructivist who sees theory as successful if it makes, rather than corresponds to, the social reality that it describes via the action of powerful agents' (Shusterman 1999: 143). And he quotes Bourdieu's claim, in *Language and Symbolic Power*, that 'It is only after Marx, and indeed only after the creation of parties capable of imposing (on a large scale) a vision of the social world according to the theory of class struggle that one could refer, strictly speaking, to classes and class struggle' (1999: 143).

How does Marx's theory of class help produce the effect it purports to describe? Marx's discourse has to convince its object (the working class) to come into (discursive) existence by setting out a version of how things might be different, and by allocat-ing to them a role in that alternative history. In other words, this involves not so much *predicting* history as helping to *make* it through a process that is very close to what Louis Althusser describes as 'interpellation'. For Althusser, identity comes into being when it is interpellated, or 'hailed', by someone in authority—for instance, when a member of the police force calls out, 'Hey you!' to someone in the street, and that person acknowledges the hailing (even if it is by running away).

Althusser's notion of interpellation provides one explanation of the relationship between theories and discourses, on the one hand, and the audiences towards which those theories were directed, on the other. But how does the audience being hailed in this way recognise itself, and its interests, in the content of a theoretical address or proposition?

To deal with this issue we have to go beyond Marx and Althusser and look at Laclau and Mouffe's neo-Marxist notion that society is 'radically indeterminate' (Laclau & Mouffe 1990: 186). What this means is that every identity in society—individual or communal—is both a kind of 'empty signifier' (a term which has no intrinsic meaning, and hence can mean anything), and the site of an agonistics (or struggle). This also applies, of course, to different social fields: the fields of sociology, philosophy and linguistics have no innate identity, but are always being transformed by struggles between groups and individuals who seek to impose their version of what the field is, and its function. Not only is the identity of a particular field always up for grabs to a certain extent but, as a corollary, so is its relation to the social and political spheres of society.

This 'constructivist' approach is certainly in evidence in Bourdieu's more recent publications such as *Free Exchange, On Television* and *Acts of Resistance*. These are texts which, as well as being written for a more general audience, actively seek to intervene in the public debate about issues such as government censorship of the arts (in the United States), the role of television and journalism in defining and constraining the public sphere (in France), and the dismantling of the welfare state (in Europe). But even Bourdieu's apparently more theoretical or academic works can be characterised in terms of this general tendency to intervene in various disciplines and fields, specifically with regard to their production of discourses and 'social reality'.

Bourdieu on Heidegger

One obvious example is his book on Heidegger, *The Political Ontology of Martin Heidegger* (1991b), which anticipated the debates (involving, among others, such eminent cultural theorists as Jacques Derrida, Jean François Lyotard, Philippe Lacoue-Labarthe and Jürgen Habermas) in the late 1980s and early 1990s about Heidegger's involvement with the Nazis, and the extent to which this involvement was reflected in, or vitiated the worth of, his work. Bourdieu's interest and involvement in this debate centred on one important point: the way in which academic fields and disciplines, in this case represented by philosophy and its intellectual issues and problems, can articulate, develop and promote conservative and/or repressive discourses, while denying any link or articulation between those discourses and the sociopolitical world. His reading of Heidegger's work in terms of this 'double key':

> revealed some of the most unforeseen political
> implications of Heideggerian philosophy: the rejection of the
> welfare state hidden at the heart of the theory of temporality,
> the anti-semitism sublimated as a condemnation of
> 'wandering', the refusal to denounce his former support of
> the Nazis inscribed in the tortuous allusions of his dialogue
> with Junger, etc. All of this could be readily found in the texts
> themselves . . . , but it stood beyond the grasp of the
> guardians of the orthodoxy of philosophical reading.
> (1992d: 152–3)

Bourdieu argues, following Marx, that supposedly neutral or apolitical fields (for instance, aesthetics and philosophy) are already implicated in the production, dissemination and naturalisation of repressive ideas and acts, and consequently provide *de facto* support for the power structures they (theoretically) ignore. Bourdieu demonstrates, in *Political Ontology*, how this kind of activity works. He identifies three stages in this process, which he holds to be more or less generic. First, Heidegger always locates and defines his arguments and discussions in terms of issues, logics and traditions that are specific to the supposedly autonomous field in which he writes (neo-Kantian thought, metaphysics, the notion of authentic being). Second, and particularly importantly, he closes off his work to political readings by employing language which is ambiguous and free of historical or social referents, and by a process of 'self-interpretation', which denies the validity of political 'translations' of his thoughts.

Finally, and as a matter of self-interest, the field (in this case, philosophy) closes ranks against political readings of Heidegger's work (labelling them vulgar, naive, unsophisticated); or alternatively, it refutes the charges of Nazism by claiming that Heidegger's work is really politically progressive. Bourdieu responds to this claim by writing, 'When I hear that "Heidegger helps us think the Holocaust", I have to believe that I am dreaming' (1992d: 153).

Bourdieu and Nietzsche

Although Bourdieu accepts that cultural fields have a role to play in the production, dissemination and authorisation of different versions of social reality, he insists that such fields are motivated and informed, first and foremost, by self-interest and internal competition—a notion he derives from Nietzsche. Bourdieu is generally cautious about the usefulness of Nietzsche's work for two main reasons. The first relates to his misgivings about 'the politically ambiguous implications of a certain way of conceiving philosophy that has spread in France since the 1960s ... especially through the exaltation of the works of Nietzsche or Heidegger, that leads to an aestheticism of transgression' (1992d: 154). The second reservation is more generic, and pertains to the notion that every theorist's usefulness is constrained by specificities of time, place and field. Bourdieu writes that:

> no matter how liberating and enlightening they may seem,
> the fulgurations and fulminations of Nietzsche against
> culture and education remain trapped within the limits
> attached to their social conditions of production, that is, to
> the position of Nietzsche in social space and, more
> specifically, within academic space. (1992d: 85)

Notwithstanding these reservations, Mitchell Aboulafia is still able to refer to 'Bourdieu's Nietzschean sensibilities with regard to interest and power' which 'allow him to develop tools to analyze power relations' (Shusterman 1999: 157). What does this mean? Whereas Marxism surveys the field of history and comes up with a single version of social and political agonistics, Nietzsche insists that there are many possible stories and developments, but these alternatives have to be repressed and forgotten so that dominant groups can justify the 'inevitability' of their own rise to power. Bourdieu uses this insight to account for the way power works (for instance in the production of meanings, the allocation of cultural capital—that is, resources which have cultural as distinct from economic value—and the transformation, rise and fall of fields), and as the basis for his understanding of human activities and practices as being largely competitive and utilitarian.

Bourdieu follows Nietzsche in understanding power as being tied up with the way in which the specific disguises itself as the general or universal—which Nietzsche refers to as the 'will to power'—much as Laclau and Mouffe understand political groups as coming to be identified with, and hence 'filling in', crucial empty signifiers such as 'the nation', 'the people', or 'the motherland'. Bourdieu writes, apropos of Nietzsche's discussion of Christianity in *The Antichrist*, that:

> Delegates [or spokespersons] *base universal value on themselves*, appropriate values, 'requisition morality', and thus monopolize the notions of God, Truth, Wisdom, People, Message, Freedom, etc. They make them synonyms. What of? Of themselves. 'I am the Truth.' They turn themselves into the sacred, they consecrate themselves and thereby draw a boundary between themselves and ordinary people. They thus become, as Nietzsche says, 'the measure of all things'. (1991a: 210–11; emphasis in original)

For both Nietzsche and Bourdieu, there is no such thing as a purely disinterested act. All activities (including the production of knowledge) are informed by the notion of self-interest to some extent, and can be contextualised with regard to the various fields in which those activities take place, and the agent's place within that field. So if we were to return to the example of Heidegger, we would read his abstracted and theoretically disinterested philosophising both 'inwardly', in terms of his competing with other philosophers and philosophical positions (Husserl, Marxism), but also 'outwardly', in terms of his (tacit) support for a certain kind of politics (Nazism). As we mentioned earlier, however, it is in Heidegger's interest (because of the way the field of philosophy works) to disguise, as far as possible, the political dimensions of his work. But it was also in his interest, at one point in German history, to support the Nazis publicly. Finally, it is also in Heidegger's interest and in the interest of the field of philosophy, as Bourdieu argues in *Political Ontology*, to keep these two interests separate from one another.

We mentioned earlier that Heidegger attempts to keep these interests separate largely by making use of a style of language (abstracted, non-referential) that seems to have little connection with the social world. This ties in with another aspect of Nietzsche's—and Wittgenstein's—work which has strongly influenced Bourdieu: both understand language not as a mirror reflecting a pre-given reality, but as a *practice* that 'makes the world', or at least determines how we understand it. Each field (medicine, philosophy, law, politics, economics) has its own set of discourses and styles of language, and that not only determines what is seen (for instance, philosophy tends to exclude the social, medicine tends to exclude abstractions), but what things are valued, what questions can be asked, and what ideas can be thought.

There is a second way in which language 'makes the world', and that is in terms of what language is 'made to mean'. While all forms of language carry their histories with them (in terms of where they have been and what they have meant), they are also in a sense empty of content: people in positions of authority within a field (such as politicians, professors, or priests), and different groups (such as businesspeople, trade unionists, or social welfare lobbyists) compete with one another in order to impose their meaning on language. And this 'politicising' of language determines how we see and understand life.

13

As Bourdieu writes: 'the obstacles to comprehension, perhaps especially when social things are in question, have less, as Wittgenstein observed, to do with the understanding than with the will' (2000: 8).

The two main notions Bourdieu takes from Nietzsche—power understood as 'will to power', with the specific disguising itself as the universal in order to acquire status and cultural capital; and language as a practice, as a way of 'making the world'—come together in what Bourdieu refers to as the 'oracle effect' (1991a: 211). He writes:

> If I, Pierre Bourdieu, a single and isolated individual, speak only for myself, say 'you must do this or that, overthrow the government or refuse Pershing missiles', who will follow me? But if I am placed in statutory conditions such that I may appear as speaking 'in the name of the masses' . . . that changes everything. (1991a: 212)

To a large extent, then, Bourdieu's understanding of human activities, and the fields in which those activities take place, is derived from Nietzsche's assertion that 'the validity of our truth claims is simply reducible to our historical interests' (Eagleton 1994: 212). Eagleton's summary of Nietzsche's position could equally apply to Bourdieu:

> For Nietzsche, all human action is a kind of fiction: it presumes some coherent, autonomous human agent (which Nietzsche regards as an illusion); implies that the beliefs and assumptions by which we act are firmly grounded (which for Nietzsche is not the case); and assumes that the effects of our actions can be rationally calculated (in Nietzsche's eyes yet another sad delusion). (1994: 212)

There is one further important aspect to this notion of the 'interestedness' of our activities which Bourdieu takes from Nietzsche and, to an equally important extent, from Sigmund Freud: all action is necessarily 'interested', but in order to look after our interests and ensure their success, we have to repress any overt sense of that interest. A politician who proposes a policy will articulate this action not in terms of potential self-advancement, but as something impersonal (doing one's duty, carrying out the public will, serving the people). Heidegger would probably describe his philosophical works not in terms of gaining fame or status within the field (and certainly not as an opportunity to push a particular political line), but as a search for truth, or as an advancement of knowledge. To put it simply, the actions of the politician (in promoting a policy) and of the philosopher (in writing a philosophical work) are only thinkable, and achievable, in terms of a narrative of self-denial. Eagleton writes, apropos of Nietzsche, that:

> To act at all means to repress or suspend . . . reflexiveness, to suffer a certain self-induced amnesia or denial. The 'true' conditions of our existence, then, must necessarily be absent from consciousness at the moment of action. This absence is . . . structural and determined, rather than a mere matter of oversight—rather as for Freud the concept of the unconscious means that the forces which determine our being cannot by definition figure within consciousness. We become conscious agents only by virtue of a certain determinate lack, repression or omission, which no amount of critical self-reflection could repair. (1994: 212–13)

This version of the unconscious is crucial to one of the central aspects of Bourdieu's work—his formulation of the notion of the habitus. The habitus constitutes Bourdieu's most ambitious attempt to ground and explain practices in terms of both specific and general sociocultural contexts, rather than in terms of the grand narratives of history (Marxism), psychoanalysis (the Oedipus Complex), structuralism (Lévi-Strauss's 'deep structures') or 'authentic being' (Heidegger). Habitus can be understood as, on the one hand, the historical and cultural production of individual practices—since contexts, laws, rules and ideologies all speak through individuals, who are never entirely aware that this is happening—and, on the other hand, the individual production of practices—since the individual always acts from self-interest.

How is the habitus tied in with the notion of the unconscious? Bourdieu describes the relationship between objective structures, subjective practices and the unconscious in the following way:

> In practice, it is the habitus, history turned into nature, i.e. denied as such, which accomplishes practically the relating of these two systems of relations, in and through the production of practice. The 'unconscious' is never anything other than the forgetting of history which history itself produces by incorporating the objective structures it produces in the second natures of the habitus. (1977a: 78–9)

Bourdieu and Pascal

For Bourdieu, the unconscious is not something that simply 'goes away' (is repressed) and occasionally 'returns' (in dreams, Freudian slips, or fetishes). Rather, it is the process that both arises out of and creates a specific, if not always deliberate, naturalising of the agendas, strategies, goals, values and desires of the habitus. This unconscious is closer to Nietzsche than to Freud precisely because it is tendentious, not only with regard to others (as in Nietzsche's example of the priest who disguises self-interest as duty), but also with regard to the self. In other words, we can only fully incorporate the habitus within the self (into the way we see things, into our bodily hexis, and into our decision making), and get on with 'serving ourselves' disguised as 'serving the people' if we suspend disbelief and truly believe without thinking, in the manner described by Pascal:

> For we must make no mistake about ourselves: we are as much automaton as mind. As a result, demonstration is not the only instrument for convincing us. How few things can be demonstrated! Proofs only convince the mind; habits provide the strongest proofs and those that are most believed. It inclines the automaton, which leads the mind unconsciously along with it. Who ever proved that it will dawn tomorrow, and that we shall die? And what is more

widely believed? It is, then, habit that convinces us and makes so many Christians. It is habit that makes Turks, heathen, trades, soldiers, etc . . . In short, we must resort to habit once the mind has seen where the truth lies, in order to steep and stain ourselves in that belief which continually eludes us, for it is too much trouble to have the proofs always present before us. We must acquire an easier belief, which is that of habit. With no violence, art or argument it makes us believe things, and so inclines all our faculties to this belief that our soul falls naturally into it. (quoted in Bourdieu 1990b: 48-9)

In *Pascalian Meditations*, which is a kind of 'self-interrogation' of Bourdieu's intellectual trajectories, dispositions, attitudes, approaches and relations to various academic fields (most particularly philosophy), he gives an account of the extent to which his work can be understood as a form of agonistics, a struggle to overcome the academic habitus and what he calls the 'scholarly disposition'. He writes:

I have never really felt justified in existing as an intellectual; and I have always tried . . . to exorcise everything in my thinking that would be linked to that status, such as philosophical intellectualism. I do not like the intellectual in myself, and what may sound, in my writing, like anti-intellectualism is chiefly directed against the intellectualism or intellectuality that remains in me, despite all my efforts. (2000: 7)

We have already discussed, in relation to Bourdieu's reading of Heidegger and his work, how the scholarly disposition 'invites' and disposes the intellectual to 'bracket off' the world. What Bourdieu is particularly (and personally) interested in, largely by way of his openly acknowledged debt to Pascal, is the process whereby the intellectual/scholarly world 'insinuates itself', along with its values and dispositions, into a practitioner's 'being'; including their bodily movements and characteristics, and ways of seeing and recognising the world. This, of course, is the same process that Bourdieu identifies with the habitus; but what he takes specifically from Pascal is what we could call the 'materialist' dimension of the habitus:

> Social reality exists, so to speak, twice, in things and in minds, in fields and in habitus, outside and inside of agents . . . the world encompasses me . . . but I comprehend it . . . precisely because it comprehends me. It is because the world has produced me, because it produces the categories of thought that I apply to it, that it appears to me as self-evident. (1992d: 127-8)

Bourdieu and 'intellectualism'

This materialist dimension of the habitus explains both Bourdieu's comments about needing to 'exorcise his intellectualism' and, more generally, the self-reflexive and peripatetic nature of his work. What Bourdieu is struggling against is the way in which day-to-day material conditions—such as sitting in an office in a grand old building, surrounded by books and other markers of scholarship, and surrounded, also, by other academics and intellectuals who dress, walk, speak and relate to each other as if they were intellectuals—'turns you', against your own inclinations, into an intellectual. This is true, of course, of all fields: working as, and in the milieu of, say, a lawyer or a street sweeper, produces both a particular kind of body and set of dispositions and values, so that the agent comes to feel, in Bourdieu's terms, 'like a fish in water' (1992d: 127).

Bourdieu's attitude towards his work, and the fields in which he operates, can be explained, to a certain extent, through his own theory of 'cultural trajectory', which can be understood as the social history that produces an agent with a particular habitus and place within a field. Bourdieu's anti-intellectualism is largely attributable to the fact that he came from the 'wrong' trajectory, so to speak. Loïc Wacquant explains it this way:

> Bourdieu's concern for reflexivity . . . is first a product of the structural discrepancy between his primary (class) habitus and that required for smooth integration into the French

academic field of the 1950s. Entering the world of intellectuals as a stranger and a misfit gave Bourdieu a definite distance from the illusions of those professors . . . The second factor is the Algerian war of liberation: it was nearly impossible, under the horrendous circumstances created by the methodical efforts of the French military to suppress Algerian nationalism, not to be constantly interpellated about the peculiar privilege of the academic who withdraws from the world in order to observe it . . . (1992d: 44–5)

Bourdieu is so critical of, and self-reflexive about, the intellectual field both because he is 'out of it', and paradoxically, because of the value he attaches to it. As he makes clear in *Pascalian Meditations*, the intellectual field (and cognate or overlapping fields such as academe and the sciences) is one of the few relatively autonomous (that is, self-regulating) fields that also carries (at least in France) considerable cultural capital and authority. This means that its agents have the ability to intervene in social issues (the dismantling of the public welfare system, racism, the domination of the public sphere by market-driven television) precisely because they are, at least theoretically, (required by the field to be) independent from political and economic influences and considerations.

Bourdieu is not so much anti-intellectual, then, as critical and wary of intellectualism; by which he means a habitus which disposes agents to retreat to their ivory towers and think and act as if the world were an idea to be contemplated and discussed, rather than a series of problems and issues affecting the everyday lives of people. As Loïc Wacquant writes again:

This is arguably the most significant difference between him [Bourdieu] and Sartre or Foucault: whereas the latter have used their intellectual capital primarily in the broader politics of society, Bourdieu has aimed his critical arsenal first and foremost at the forms of tyranny—in Pascal's sense—that threaten the intellectual field itself. (1992d: 56)

Conclusion

- Bourdieu follows Marx, Pascal and Wittgenstein in viewing scholarly work, and 'cultural production' in general, as interventions in the social world, rather than a form of disinterested reflection.
- As a corollary he accepts that our activities and practices, while being disguised as disinterested, or a form of duty, are both self-interested and political; that is to say, they are predicated on what Nietzsche calls the 'will to power'.

These two insights inform both the kinds of directions Bourdieu's work takes, and what he makes of the disciplinary knowledge of fields such as linguistics, philosophy and anthropology. In our next chapter we will look at how Bourdieu uses these two insights in theorising three of his most influential concepts, capital, field and habitus.

Further reading

Bourdieu, Pierre 1991, *The Political Ontology of Martin Heidegger*, Polity Press, Cambridge

Bourdieu, Pierre 2000, *Pascalian Meditations*, Polity Press, Cambridge

Calhoun, Craig et al. (eds) 1993, *Bourdieu: Critical Perspectives*, University of Chicago Press, Chicago

Fowler, Bridget 1997, *Pierre Bourdieu and Cultural Theory: Critical Investigations*, Sage, London

Lane, Jeremy 2000, *Pierre Bourdieu: A Critical Introduction*, Pluto Press, London

Swartz, David 1997, *Culture and Power: The Sociology of Pierre Bourdieu*, University of Chicago Press, Chicago

2

Cultural field and the habitus

In our previous chapter we described some of the theoretical ideas, attitudes and perspectives that have influenced and informed Bourdieu's work. In the next two chapters we look at how Bourdieu has tried to understand and explain the relationship between people's practices and the contexts in which those practices occur. Bourdieu refers to these contexts—discourses, institutions, values, rules and regulations—which produce and transform attitudes and practices as 'cultural fields'. In the first part of this chapter we identify and describe how cultural fields operate, through reference to notions such as cultural capital, universalisation, illusio, symbolic violence and misrecognition. In the second part we look at how Bourdieu arrives at the notion of the habitus, first through his critique of subjectivist and objectivist accounts of human activity, and then by thinking beyond these two accounts to produce what he calls a 'double historicity' of practice. We will also look at the different aspects that Bourdieu ascribes to the habitus, such as disposition and trajectory, its unconscious dimension, and the various ways it comes to be embodied.

Cultural field and capital

A cultural field can be defined as a series of institutions, rules, rituals, conventions, categories, designations, appointments and titles which constitute an objective hierarchy, and which produce and authorise certain discourses and activities. But it is also constituted by, or out of, the conflict which is involved when groups or individuals attempt to determine what constitutes capital within that field, and how that capital is to be distributed. Bourdieu understands the concept of cultural field to refer to fluid and dynamic, rather than static, entities. Cultural fields, that is, are made up not simply of institutions and rules, but of the interactions between institutions, rules and practices.

What do we understand by the term 'cultural capital'? Richard Harker, Cheleen Mahar and Chris Wilkes, in their book *An Introduction to the Work of Pierre Bourdieu* (1990), make the point that:

> the definition of capital is very wide for Bourdieu and includes material things (which can have symbolic value), as well as 'untouchable' but culturally significant attributes such as prestige, status and authority (referred to as symbolic capital), along with cultural capital (defined as culturally-valued taste and consumption patterns) . . . For Bourdieu, capital acts as a social relation within a system of exchange, and the term is extended 'to all the goods, material and symbolic, without distinction, that present themselves as rare and worthy of being sought after in a particular social formation'. (Harker et al. 1990: 1)

It is important to remember that cultural capital is not set in stone or universally accepted, either within or across fields. In business, for instance, a corporation might advertise itself as a 'family company', in order to increase or maintain their share of the market. The positive capital associated with such a move is that it personalises the company. A television commercial for Dilmah Tea, for instance, shows the head of the company sitting at a table on a tea plantation with his two sons ('my boys'), who will one day take over the company and run it 'just like Dad'. The point here is to make a particular product attractive by associating it with supposedly familial and other 'agreeable' values (commitment, continuity, caring, loyalty). In different circumstances, however, designating oneself as a 'family company' might constitute negative capital: in an increasingly globalised

22

economy, it might connote insularity, a lack of ambition, or anachronistic values (because businesses are about profits, not relationships).

The amount of power a person has within a field depends on that person's position within the field, and the amount of capital she or he possesses. Of course, one of the advantages of being in a position of power is that it enables groups or agents to designate what is 'authentic' capital. Generally, the value or otherwise of specific forms of capital is determined within, and often confined to, a particular field—although overlapping does occur.

Reproduction and transformation

Bourdieu explains the competition for capital within fields with reference to two terms, reproduction and transformation. By and large, agents adjust their expectations with regard to the capital they are likely to attain in terms of the 'practical' limitations imposed upon them by their place in the field, their educational background, social connections, class position and so forth. Consequently—and to a certain extent, paradoxically—those with the least amount of capital tend to be less ambitious, and more 'satisfied' with their lot; in Bourdieu's terms, 'the subjective hope of profit tends to be adjusted to the objective probability of profit' (2000: 216). What this leads to is a reproduction of symbolic domination: what Bourdieu describes as:

> the realistic, even resigned or fatalistic, dispositions which lead members of the dominated classes to put up with objective conditions that would be judged intolerable or revolting by agents otherwise disposed . . . help to reproduce the conditions of oppression. (2000: 217)

Of course, this does not stop agents from 'gambling' for capital in order to improve their place within a field. A lowly academic who picks up a job writing a column for a 'respectable' daily newspaper, for instance, could suddenly gain capital (widespread public recognition, status as a commentator on social issues, becoming a regular 'contact' for media enquiries) that can transform both their own value and place within the field, and ultimately (if this form of capital 'caught on'), even the field itself. Families from migrant communities will often put all their resources into educating one or more of their children in order to effect a similar transformation (in this case, a move from one class position to another).

Bourdieu insists, however, that this kind of 'gambling' is largely doomed to failure. Although a lower class migrant family may strive to get its children educated, the habitus of the children will, in advance, disqualify them from success, both in the sense that the children will signal, in everything they do and say, their unsuitability for higher education, and as a corollary, the children will themselves recognise this, and more or less expect failure. As Bourdieu writes: 'Those who talk of equality of opportunity forget that social games . . . are not "fair games". Without being, strictly speaking, rigged, the competition resembles a handicap race that has lasted for generations' (2000: 214–15).

An example of these different relations and processes comes from the field of sport. Theoretically, this should be the most straightforward and transparent of all fields. After all, sport is supposed to be about competition and fair play, and one would expect that capital would be apportioned according to simple criteria (for instance, winning and losing, or playing in the 'right spirit'). But this is not, and never really has been, the case. At one stage—certainly in the nineteenth century, and possibly well into the twentieth century—sport was relatively autonomous. That is to say, generally speaking its identity and capital were not determined by other powerful fields such as business or government. Rather, like all fields, it reproduced itself in terms of four main modes of operation: what Bourdieu would call misrecognition, symbolic violence, illusio and universalisation.

Misrecognition and symbolic violence

Bourdieu understands misrecognition as a 'form of forgetting' that agents are caught up in, and produced by. He writes:

> The agent engaged in practice knows the world . . . too well, without objectifying distance, takes it for granted, precisely because he is caught up in it, bound up with it; he inhabits it like a garment . . . he feels at home in the world because the world is also in him, in the form of the habitus (2000: 142–3)

Misrecognition is the key to what Bourdieu calls the function of 'symbolic violence', which he defines as 'the violence which is exercised upon a social agent with his or her complicity' (1992d: 167). In other words, agents are subjected to forms of violence (treated as inferior, denied resources, limited in their social mobility and aspirations), but they do not perceive it that way; rather, their situation seems to them to be 'the natural order of things'. One of the more obvious examples of the relation between misrecognition and symbolic violence can be seen in the way gender relations have, historically, been defined in terms of male domination. Every aspect of women's bodies and activities was 'imprisoned', to some extent, by the workings of the habitus. Female bodies were both read as having significance which demonstrated their inferiority (they were weak, soft, unfit for hard work, unable to take pressure), and were inculcated (at home, school, church) with a 'bodily hexis that constitutes a veritable embodied politics' (1992d: 172).

Patriarchy, in this account, cannot be understood simply in terms of a coercion by one group (men) of another (women). Rather, we can say that gender domination took (and takes) place precisely because women misrecognised the symbolic violence to which they were subjected as something that was natural, simply 'the way of the world'. Consequently they were complicit in the production of those things (bodily performances, for instance) which worked to reinscribe their domination. Of course, as cultures change, there is always the prospect that men can be caught up in the same form of imprisonment; that is, maintain an attachment to certain performances of masculinity which are no longer acceptable or functional, and thus counterproductive.

Misrecognition also helps us make sense of the double-dealing strategies whereby leaders, managers, officials or delegates of a field appear to be acting in a disinterested or principled manner 'for the field' and its values. So in sport, the legendary American, Avery Brundage, could rule over his domain (the Olympic movement) as a patriarch who had the best interests of the game at heart. In effect he was ensuring that the field and its practices reflected his own values. As a result, the sub-field of athletics and its practices, rules, discourses and forms of capital corresponded to a logic that was clearly political and sectarian (in Brundage's case, upper class values), but which had to be treated as inextricably linked to, and in fact derived from, the field itself. Brundage, for example, hated professionalism in sport, and restricted the Olympics, ostensibly, to amateurs. But of course the best athletes invariably received remuneration (from governments, sports departments, sponsors, organisers). Everyone knew what was happening, but everyone pretended that athletes were still amateurs. The real scandal was not in accepting money; it was either getting caught or telling the truth about what became known as 'shamateurism'.

Illusio and universalisation

This more or less unthinking commitment to the logic, values and capital of a field corresponds to what Bourdieu calls 'illusio', which is:

> the fact of being caught up in and by the game, of believing ... that playing is worth the effort ..., to participate, to admit that the game is worth playing and that the stakes created in and through the fact of playing are worth pursuing; it is to recognise the game and to recognise its stakes. When you read, in Saint-Simon, about the quarrel of hats (who should bow first), if you were not born in a court society, if you do not possess the habitus of a person of the court, if the structures of the game are not also in your mind, the quarrel will seem ridiculous and futile to you. (1998d: 76–7)

The illusio of the (apparently meaningless) quarrel of the hats is similar to what happened in the Olympic movement with the games that the Olympic movement played over amateurism, which became known as shamateurism. The rules of amateurism forbade athletes from accepting cash for sporting performances. On the other hand there was nothing to stop athletes from receiving travelling expenses, having equipment supplied for free, or from working in highly paid government or corporate jobs that never required their presence. In effect the Olympic movement under Brundage lived out the illusio of their passionate commitment to keeping athletics 'pure', while tacitly allowing most of the best athletes to earn their living as professionals. The situation was best summed up by a sportsman from a field with a similar attachment to shamateurism—tennis. When the Spanish amateur champion Manuel Santana was asked, privately, why he did not turn professional, he replied that he couldn't afford the drop in salary.

Under Brundage the Olympic movement represented itself and its 'lily-white' values as the only true manifestation of the undiluted essence of sport. That is to say, it tried to universalise itself so that its values would become synonymous with the field as a whole. The so-called 'Olympic ideals', which emphasise disinterested values ('sport for sport's sake'), were reproduced by governments, the media, bureaucrats, sports administrators and teachers as criteria (capital) for differentiating 'true' sportspeople. This had a number of manifestations. In the United States in the first half of the twentieth century, professional American football received very little media coverage or public attention compared to (supposedly) amateur college football. And amateur tennis players who won tournaments like Wimbledon became national heroes, while the professional circuit, dubbed 'a circus', was more or less ignored by the media. In both cases the professionals were much better sportspeople than those in the amateur ranks, but this did not translate into cultural (or even economic) capital.

The Olympic movement's attempts to universalise its values and capital were not, of course, universally successful. In some sub-fields (such as golf, soccer and boxing), professionals were generally accorded a higher status, and received more media and public attention, than amateurs. And in rugby league (a sport played predominantly in the north of Britain and eastern

Australia), professionalism became the means by which the sport and its working class fans distinguished themselves from a rival code (rugby union) and its supporters (the upper classes).

But even where a sport was clearly professional (golf, soccer, boxing, rugby league), its core values and discourses—what Bourdieu would call its 'doxa'—were usually articulated (by the media, officials, and by sportspersons giving interviews) as being tied to the notion of 'sport for sport's sake'. This is another example of illusio: although by the middle of the last century many sports were operating on a professional basis (soccer in Europe and South America, golf and tennis in the United States and Europe), most members of the field were still 'spoken' by the discourses of what we might call 'inalienable sport'.

Inalienable culture and the market

When we refer to sport as 'inalienable', we mean that it was supposedly above the values of the marketplace. Soccer players earned high salaries, and were treated—and sold—by clubs as a form of commodity. But if an English soccer star in the 1950s were interviewed about his reasons for playing the game, he would invariably cite a number of motivations—glory, representing his country, helping his teammates, pleasing the local supporters, even just having fun, all of which might be true. What he could not say, however, was that he was doing it for the money; that would have automatically earned him the contempt and anger of the fans and everyone else in the field. The only capital that a soccer player could legitimately refer to was inalienable cultural capital such as international honour, longevity, skill, loyalty to a team or town, toughness or a sense of fair play.

Cultural fields themselves are not autonomous, or uninfluenced by other fields. We made the point that fields are fluid and dynamic, mainly because they are always being changed both by internal practices and politics, and by their convergence with other fields. Again, sport can serve as an example of both these dynamic tendencies. The notion that the field of sport was 'inalienable' with regard to economic considerations changed very quickly from the 1960s onward, basically as the result of a combination of internal and external pressures: what Bourdieu would call the transformation of an autonomous field into a heteronomous one. An external pressure was that the field of business began to intrude more openly into the field of sport. Initially this came in the form of increased sponsorship and television involvement, but more recently it has manifested itself in the listing of sporting teams (European soccer teams, for instance) as companies on the stock exchange. An internal pressure has come about as different sports organisations have been taken over by officials (Juan Samaranch with regard to the Olympic movement, Primo Nebiolo for international athletics, and Joao Havelange for international soccer) whose primary aim has been to 'corporatise' their sport to the fullest.

The internal and external changes that largely transformed sport from the 1960s onward were of course complementary, as is the case with all fields. External convergences, such as the increased interconnectedness of sport with the field of business and its greater reliance on that field, gave rise to opportunities for internal change. Officials and players who were able to seize the day and run with business invariably increased their own capital (and power), and brought most of the field with them. Officials (and their sports) who refused to 'play the new game' were increasingly isolated, and left behind.

This had a rolling effect: the more business invested in, and controlled, certain sports, the more those chosen sports (American football, English soccer, tennis, golf, the Olympics) prospered in terms of media publicity, attendances, sponsorship and players' wages. At the same time the doxa of 'sport for sport's sake' became more tenuous, with notions such as loyalty (of players to teams, and teams to localities) being replaced by unabashed economic considerations. In English soccer, for instance, players frequently make public demands for increased wages as a condition of their continuing 'interest', and in the United States American football owners threaten to relocate to another city unless local councils meet their financial demands.

It is important to point out that the transformation of a field, whether it is dramatic or gradual, does not occur in a consistent or homogeneous fashion. Certain sub-sections or even pockets of a field may embrace the transformation of the field much more quickly. As a result, that field is usually 'traumatised' by fairly overt disagreements and agonistics, primarily over which part most truly represents or embodies the field and its values. If we stay with the field of sport we can find numerous examples of this phenomenon, particularly in areas that have lagged behind these changes.

A good example is Australian sport, which for most of the twentieth century was able to embrace professionalism to a qualified extent (in sports such as rugby league, Australian rules football and soccer), while maintaining a strong discursive and practical commitment to the ethos of sport's inalienability, particularly through an emphasis on its 'tribal' nature (that is, teams were closely associated with classes, suburbs or other communities). However, in the 1990s the two main football codes—rugby league and Australian rules—became increasingly corporatised; and as a consequence the rituals, traditions and ethos of those games began to give way to business decisions. Seemingly inviolate traditions such as the design of team jumpers, the time and day for playing matches, and even the viability of teams were changed to accommodate sponsors and television. This has resulted in an ongoing battle, played out in newspapers, television, radio, public rallies and in the courts, between those representing the tradition of a field supposedly 'of and for itself' (that is, relatively autonomous and above the market), and those who see the sport as a corporate activity.

The transformation of a particular field always results in concomitant transformations or modifications of the identity of members of the field. One of the more interesting aspects of the 'agonistics' that currently characterises different sports in Australia is the way in which it impinges upon individual identities, practices, dispositions and values. Some people condemned the corporatisation of their sport, and strongly resisted it, even when it went against their own economic interests. Others, who were originally closely associated with, and championed, the inalienable ethos of their sport were also able to change identities, and move from being sportspeople to businesspeople without too much trouble.

Much the same has happened to the identity of players in all sports, but most particularly in those that have been thoroughly corporatised. Prior to the 1960s, a sportsperson's identity was strongly informed, at least at a discursive, public level, by a strong commitment to the game and its values (that is, an attachment to fair play, loyalty, selflessness, the good of the game) and supposedly 'masculine' qualities such as strength, determination, discipline, courage, tolerance of pain. With the advent of corporatisation, sporting identities were influenced by a different form of commoditisation which emphasised and valued (or at least didn't negatively value) individuality, selfishness, arrogance, a lack of discipline, disrespect for authority, sexuality and most importantly, an ability to create headlines or initiate scandals.

Figures such as George Best, Diego Maradona and David Beckham in soccer, John McEnroe, Illie Nastase and, more recently, Anna Kournikova in tennis, Joe Namath in American football, Jose Canseco in baseball and, most famously, Dennis Rodman in basketball were viewed and treated more like pop stars than sportspersons. And crowds would turn up, not necessarily to see them exhibit sporting skills, but because of their penchants for excessive behaviour (McEnroe, Nastase, Rodman), their sexual attractiveness or notoriety (Namath, Kournikova, Beckham, Rodman), or because of their 'larger than life' reputations (Canseco, Namath, Rodman). Even the masculinist character of sporting identity has been replaced, to a certain extent: Rodman's cross-dressing and Beckham's reported penchant for wearing his wife's underwear are symptomatic of this.

Habitus and objectivism/subjectivism

We pointed out in Chapter 1 that Bourdieu had a tendency to pick up on theoretical conundrums or debates that characterise a field, and transform them; and this is very much the case with his notions of habitus. Most of the fields in which Bourdieu has worked, such as sociology, anthropology, ethnography and linguistics, have been split between objectivist and subjectivist explanations of human practice. In his introduction to *The Logic of Practice*, Bourdieu writes that 'Of all the oppositions that artificially divide social science, the most fundamental, and the most ruinous, is the one that is set up between subjectivism and objectivism' (1990b: 25). The notions of cultural field and the habitus were 'created' by Bourdieu primarily as a means of thinking beyond this subjectivist–objectivist split.

What do the terms 'subjectivist' and 'objectivist' actually mean? Loïc Wacquant describes subjectivism, or the subjectivist point of view, as that which:

> asserts that social reality is a 'contingent ongoing accomplishment' of competent social actors who continually construct their social world via 'the organized artful practices of everyday life' . . . Through the lens of this social phenomenology, society appears as the emergent product of the decisions, actions, and cognitions of conscious, alert individuals to whom the world is given as immediately familiar and meaningful. (1992d: 9)

The most prevalent and recognisable example of this way of thinking in popular culture is the conventional hero of Hollywood films. Think of any Arnold Schwarzenegger film (for instance, *Predator*, *Total Recall*, *True Lies*) and the characters he plays in them: they are usually in control of their ideas, thoughts and behaviour, and they determine their environment through the strength of their will and their physical prowess, much more than their environment (in the form of the government, bureaucracies, conventional wisdom) determines them. In fact in most of Schwarzenegger's films (and in action films starring actors such as Sylvester Stallone and Bruce Willis) the story is really about the battle between the individual hero who is courageous, strong, principled and free thinking, and his environment which is invariably bureaucratic, deterministic, dehumanised, corrupted and narrow minded.

Bourdieu accepts that subjectivism is useful in that it draws attention to the ways in which agents, at a practical, everyday level, negotiate various attempts (by governments, bureaucracies, institutions, capitalism) to tell them what to do, how to behave, and how to think. In other words it serves as an antidote to those

Marxist theories (associated with the Frankfurt School) which presume that people are 'cultural dupes' mindlessly consuming the ideologies of government and capitalism. But Bourdieu rejects the subjectivist approach because it fails to take into account the close connection between the objective structures of a culture, which include the values, ideas, desires and narratives produced by, and characteristic of, cultural institutions such as the family, religious groups, education systems and government bodies, on the one hand, and the specific tendencies, activities, values and dispositions of individuals, on the other.

Objectivism is useful for Bourdieu because it allows him to decode 'the unwritten musical score according to which the actions of agents, each of whom believes she is improvising her own melody, are organized' (1992d: 8). The best known body of objectivist theory is structuralism, which was practiced in, and influenced, just about every major humanities and social sciences discipline, including linguistics (Saussure and Jakobson), anthropology (Lévi-Strauss), literature (the Russian Formalists), cultural studies (Barthes), Marxism (Althusser) and psychoanalysis (Lacan).

There are three main insights which Bourdieu takes from structuralism, and which clearly influenced his notions of cultural field and the habitus. First, structuralist accounts of practice start from the premise that people more or less reproduce the objective structures of the society, culture or community they live in, and which are articulated in terms of ideas, values, documents, policies, rituals, discourses, relations, myths and dispositions. The catch cry of structuralism was Lévi-Strauss' observation that 'myths think in men, unbeknown to them' (Hawkes 1997: 41). In other words, while people think that they are employing various modes of communication ('sign systems' such as written and spoken language, or bodily gestures), in fact those sign systems produce them, and their activities, thoughts and desires.

Second, sign systems not only 'think' people into existence; they also determine how they perceive the world. What this means is that 'reality' is both produced and delimited by whatever sign systems we have at our disposal. In contemporary society we perceive and understand people aged, say thirteen years and under, in terms of the word 'child'. This connotes a number of things, including distinguishing that person from an adult. But as the French historian Philippe Aries has pointed out, what we understand by that word did not exist in the sixteenth century; up to then twelve-year-olds would have been viewed and treated as miniature adults.

The third point Bourdieu takes from structuralism is the notion of relational thinking. Reality and people are 'processed' through the meaning machines that constitute our sign systems; but the signs in those systems mean nothing in themselves; they only 'mean' insofar as they are part of a sign system, and can be related to other signs in that system. For instance, the term 'Coca Cola' does not derive its meaning from any real thing that is out there in the world. Rather, we understand 'Coca Cola' in relation to other terms, called 'binaries' ('Coca Cola' means, among other things, not 'Pepsi', not 'Perrier', not 'yak juice').

These three points can be summed up as follows:

- objective structures produce people, their subjectivities, their worldview; and, as a consequence
- they also produce what people come to know as the 'reality' of the world; and
- every thing, object and idea within a culture only has meaning in relation to other elements in that culture.

Structuralism can be understood, then, as a form of objectivism which:

> sets out to establish objective regularities (structures, laws, systems of relationships, etc.) independent of individual consciousness and wills. ... It raises, objectively at least, the forgotten question of the particular conditions which make doxic experience of the social world possible. (Bourdieu 1990b: 26)

But this emphasis on the deterministic aspect of human practice is, for Bourdieu, both a strength and a weakness. Objectivism can see practice only as the reproduction of structures, and no more.

Perhaps the most obvious example of this shortcoming in objectivist readings of practice is to be found in the activities of anthropologists when they are investigating, describing analysing and explaining so-called 'primitive' or 'native' cultures.

Bourdieu himself did anthropological work in Algeria in the 1960s, and he was struck by the incongruous, even comical aspect of anthropologists seeking out so-called primitive cultures, then observing, recording, describing, questioning and evaluating what was going on in front of them, in order to bring it all back home as fresh anthropological knowledge. Bourdieu had problems with this kind of activity for two reasons. First, just as subjectivist accounts of practice edit out, and even repress, the relationship between cultural structures and individual practices, objectivist accounts of 'other' practices or cultures, such as those engaged in by anthropologists, have no place for the forgotten question of the particular conditions which make, say, anthropology possible. In other words, in order for an anthropologist to objectify another culture as primitive, that anthropologist must naturalise the values that characterise one culture as civilised or advanced, and another culture as its opposite.

Anthropologists observing other cultures have, to a certain extent, already written their books before they arrive. Designating a culture as primitive is a form of (usually negative) evaluation which determines, to no small extent, what questions the anthropologists will ask, what things they will see and miss, and what aspects they will emphasise as important, or as the keys to the culture. Anthropologists objectify other peoples, but they invariably fail to objectify their own practices.

The second major difficulty Bourdieu has with objectivist accounts of cultures and practices is that he sees them as failing to understand that descriptions of objective regularities (That is, structures, laws, systems) do not tell us how people use—inhabit, negotiate, or elude—those objective regularities.

An example of this point is to be found in the John Carpenter film *Starman*, which demonstrates how the difference between laws and practices is forgotten—or repressed—by practitioners. In the film an alien, played by Jeff Bridges, is travelling across the United States by car with a woman played by Karen Allen.

The woman does all the driving until Bridges points out that he has been closely observing her driving the car, has analysed and taken in all the rules and skills involved, and would like to drive himself. Allen reluctantly agrees, but almost immediately Bridges runs a red light and only narrowly avoids an accident. Allen abuses him, but Bridges replies that, after watching her drive, he had concluded that the rules about road lights were as follows: green means go fast, orange means go slightly faster, and red means go very fast.

Subjectivism and objectivism remain useful notions in attempting to account for practice, mainly because they point to the shortcomings of their 'other'. Subjectivism draws attention to the point that objectivist maps of a culture (such as laws, rules, and systems) edit out intentionality and individuality (or what is referred to as 'agency'). Objectivism points out that individuality and intentionality are regulated by cultural contexts—that is, we can only 'intend' what is available to us within a culture.

Bourdieu, reading across both subjectivist and objectivist approaches simultaneously, insists that practice is always informed by a sense of agency (the ability to understand and control our own actions), but that the possibilities of agency must be understood and contextualised in terms of its relation to the objective structures of a culture—what he refers to, generally, as cultural fields. For Bourdieu this relationship between field and habitus does not completely determine people's actions and thoughts, but no practice is explicable without reference to them.

Habitus and bodily hexis

Bourdieu refers to the partly unconscious 'taking in' of rules, values and dispositions as 'the habitus', which he defines as 'the durably installed generative principle of regulated improvisations . . . [which produces] practices' (1977a: 78). In other words, habitus can be understood as the values and dispositions gained from our cultural history that generally stay with us across contexts (they are durable and transposable). These values and dispositions allow us to respond to cultural rules and contexts in a variety of ways (because they allow for improvisations), but the responses are always largely determined—regulated—by where (and who) we have been in a culture.

We pointed out in Chapter 1 that Bourdieu's 'anti-intellectualism' could be understood as an attempt to free himself, as far as was possible, from aspects of the intellectual or academic habitus. As agents move through and across different fields, they tend to incorporate into their habitus the values and imperatives of those fields. And this is most clearly demonstrated in the way the relationship between field and habitus functions to 'produce' agent's bodies and bodily dispositions: what Bourdieu refers to as the 'bodily hexis'. We may think of the body as something individual, as subject to, belonging to, and characteristic of, the self. But, as Bourdieu points out, this notion of the 'individual, self-contained body' is also a product of the habitus:

> this body which indisputably functions as the principle of individuation . . ., ratified and reinforced by the legal definition of the individual as an abstract, interchangeable being . . . [is] open to the world, and therefore exposed to the world, and so capable of being conditioned by the world, shaped by the material and cultural conditions of existence in which it is placed from the beginning . . . (2000: 133–4)

We referred, in Chapter 1, to academics cloistered in their 'ivory towers', who are disposed by their physical milieu (libraries, book-filled offices, lecture theatres) and spatial location (the university is a kind of 'world within itself', set apart from the rest of society) to 'bracket off' the rest of the world. This disposition manifests itself, however, not just in attitudes, approaches and values (real problems are made 'academic', and treated as abstractions), but in terms of the production of an 'intellectual body'. If you look at any number of jackets of academic books, you will find the author 'arranged' and posed in particular ways (a sombre expression, hands on chin, wearing glasses) which are meant to connote, say, seriousness, or a contemplative state of mind.

Much the same process can be seen with regard to the field of sport. Sportspeople, of course, are expected to have strongly exercised and finely honed bodies, which fit as closely as possible to the demands of their particular discipline (a rugby body, for instance, is very different from the body of a distance runner). What is particularly interesting, however, is what happens when sportspeople move into different fields, such as public relations or the media, where there is no 'coincidence' between their bodies and their new work. The overwhelming impression, in most cases (although sportspeople are now tutored in, say, working with the media) is of awkwardness, not just in what to say or when to say it, but in the relationship between their bodies and their new surrounds (where and how to move, facial expressions, when to laugh). They appear, that is, like fish out of water.

Aspects of the habitus

There are a number of further points that Bourdieu associates with habitus. First, knowledge (the way we understand the world, our beliefs and values) is always constructed through the habitus, rather than being passively recorded. Second, we are disposed towards certain attitudes, values or ways of behaving because of the influence exerted by our cultural trajectories. These dispositions are transposable across fields. Third, the habitus is always constituted in moments of practice. It is always 'of the moment', brought out when a set of dispositions meets a particular problem, choice or context. In other words, it can be understood as a 'feel for the game' that is everyday life. Finally, habitus operates at a level that is at least partly unconscious. Why? Because habitus is, in a sense, entirely arbitrary; there is nothing natural or essential about the values we hold, the desires we pursue, or the practices in which we engage.

This is not to say that these arbitrary practices are unmotivated, and that we act out of disinterestedness. On the contrary, and as we pointed out with regard to the field of sport, all practices are informed by notions of power, politics and self-interest. But in order for a particular habitus to function smoothly and effectively, individuals must normally think that the possibilities from which they choose are in fact necessities, common sense, natural or inevitable. Other possibilities are ruled out precisely because they are unthinkable.

The rules and structures of perception that pertain to a particular habitus are inscribed on, and in, individuals as if they were 'human nature' or 'civilised behaviour', and things outside those rules and structures are usually understood, when forced upon us, as amounting to the horrific and barbaric, or the absurd and comic. An example of how arbitrary structures and rules are produced as a naturalised habitus can be seen in western meat-eating patterns. Cows, pigs, chickens, ducks, turkeys and sheep are all slaughtered, packaged and consumed as staple components of a western diet, while domestic animals such as cats, dogs and hamsters are (unconsciously) excluded from this category. When stories circulate about foreigners eating cats or dogs, the usual response is one of disgust and incomprehension.

What is implicit in this reaction is the notion that it is proper to eat some animals because they are 'depersonalised' (we have herds of cattle and flocks of sheep, but not hordes of hamsters); and we often reinforce this act of depersonalisation by naming the meat differently from the animal (we eat beef, not cow; mutton, not sheep). Animals which we personalise and regard as pets, on the other hand, are almost impossible to think of as food. Imagine, if you can, an English monarchist, starving in the wilderness, faced with the prospect of having to eat a 'royal' corgi to survive. Cannibalism might be a more palatable option.

Systems, rules, laws, structures and categories of meaning and perception can only function effectively as habitus if we do not think about the specific sociocultural conditions or contexts of their production and existence: or what Bourdieu calls 'the forgetting of history which history itself produces' (1990b: 56). An example of this is history itself—or, more specifically, the way in which the teaching of history in the West (particularly in schools) has edited out the political, artistic, philosophical and scientific achievements of Islamic cultures from the sixth century to the present. The term 'the Dark Ages' has been used, for instance, to describe the period of the Islamic military and cultural eclipse of the west. What this term implies, and the perception it creates, is that non-western societies are effectively irrelevant, or at least incapable of producing 'civilisation'. Equally importantly, this version of history effectively universalises western experience, with the conventional narrative points of western history (Greece, Rome, Christianity, the Renaissance, the age of exploration, the Enlightenment, the Industrial age) coming to refer to, and incorporate, the history of all peoples. New historical details (for instance, the recent discovery of evidence of metal work in Southeast Asia which challenges the notion that the fertile crescent was the 'cradle of civilisation') can modify the western narrativisation of human history, while still leaving it more or less intact.

The most crucial aspect of habitus, then, is that it naturalises itself and the cultural rules, agendas and values that make it possible. But there are also a number of other important points that can be identified in Bourdieu's definition. First, conditioning associated with a particular type of existence, based on shared cultural trajectories, produces the habitus. Now this can seem a difficult notion, because we are not talking about something as straightforward as, say, the Marxist idea of class categories based on positions occupied within the economic sphere. Habitus is certainly informed by, without being entirely explicable in terms of, class affiliations.

An example of this occurs in the British comedy series *Blackadder*. The fourth and final series is set in World War I, with assorted members of the British army awaiting the order to advance towards the German lines. The troops are more or less divided into two groups: those in the trenches who are involved in the fighting (and who will be killed), and those behind the lines giving orders (who will not be killed). Now, throughout the series clear delineations are drawn between different groups in terms of class. General Melchett and Lieutenant George, for instance, both come from upper-class, private school backgrounds, and share values, social connections, and banter which is incomprehensible to lower- and middle-class characters such as Baldrick and Blackadder. General Melchett, who gives orders from behind the lines ('Remember men', says the general, 'we're right behind you'. 'Yes', says Blackadder, 'about three miles behind us'), is enthusiastic about the war, and oblivious to the dangers involved. Curiously, despite being in the trenches and having to eat rats, sleep in puddles and be shot at by the Germans, Lieutenant George shares the general's views—at least at first. In fact one of the more obviously comic aspects of the series is the way in which George is able to maintain his class disposition and its concomitant discourses (which reduces the war to a kind of school game, involving 'giving Harry Hun six of the best, trousers down') despite the mounting evidence of the absurdity of this position, and the danger to his life.

George is clearly 'written' by his class habitus to the extent that he is effectively blind to what is happening around him. However, after his upper-class friends have all been slaughtered and his own death becomes inevitable, he undergoes an ever-so-subtle transformation. As the four soldiers—the lower-class Baldrick, the middle-class Blackadder and Darling, and the upper-class George—prepare to charge suicidally towards the enemy guns, they speak with one mind about not wanting to die. In that moment, George's acceptance and naive (mis)understanding of the war is replaced—too late—by fear and disbelief. In other words, George finally throws off his upper-class-based belief in the war, and briefly takes on the habitus—shared by Blackadder and Baldrick—of a soldier at the front.

The important point here is that the habitus is both durable, and oriented towards the practical: dispositions, knowledges and values are always potentially subject to modification, rather than being passively consumed or reinscribed. This occurs when the narratives, values and explanations of a habitus no longer make sense, as is the case with Lieutenant George; or again, when agents use their understanding and feel for the rules of the game as a means of furthering and improving their own standing and capital within a cultural field. It must be stressed, however, that such 'interests' are themselves produced by, and through, the habitus.

This is also played out in *Blackadder* where two characters, Captains Blackadder and Darling (both middle-class), attempt to avoid, from the very beginning, the perils of trench warfare. They each have a different way of doing this: Blackadder schemes to get posted to Paris, or Tahiti, or London; while Darling works as

41

a bureaucrat at headquarters (Private Baldrick proposes to survive, rather less realistically, by dressing up as a woman and marrying General Melchett). Their intentions are not to overthrow or challenge the 'game', or to intervene in what is clearly a morally indefensible situation: rather, they just want to avoid what is happening to everyone else at the front (that is, death). They do not believe in the game, but they continue to define their interests within its parameters, narratives and values by serving the war effort.

Habitus always makes a 'virtue out of necessity'. This means that just because there is a close relationship between 'objective probabilities (for example, the chances of access to a particular good) and agents' subjective aspirations ("motivations" and "needs")' (Bourdieu 1990b: 54), people do not necessarily make those kinds of calculations and decisions freely, uninfluenced by habitus. On the contrary, Bourdieu makes the point that those decisions are always already made: 'The most improbable practices are therefore excluded, as unthinkable, by a kind of immediate submission to order that inclines agents to make a virtue of necessity, that is, to refuse what is anyway denied and to will the inevitable' (1990b: 54).

The decisions taken by Captains Blackadder and Darling correspond to this 'logic of the habitus'; unlike Baldrick, they understand that they will never be admitted into the upper class, through marriage or any other means. They calculate that the best they can do to achieve safety is to perform 'usefulness' with regard to the war effort. This will not stop the killing (in fact, it will effectively perpetuate it), but it is their best chance to avoid being killed.

What these examples from *Blackadder* and our earlier examples from the field of sport point to is that while the habitus is subject to modification and even change, such a process is usually gradual (an exception would be something like Paul of Tarsus' dramatic conversion from a persecutor of Christians to Christian zealot—but then God apparently had something to do with that). The habitus can tolerate social upheavals, and agents moving from one field to another, because there is a 'continuity of meaning' (or a doxa) that characterises and even permeates most national cultures, and is usually promoted by governments, bureaucracies, the media and education systems.

Habitus and globalisation

The anthropologist Arjun Appadurai has raised the question, however, as to the effect that the forces and processes of globalisation have on the habitus. Appadurai suggests that the more or less unregulated flow of cultural texts, in concert with the continuous 'flowing of peoples' that characterises the contemporary world, works to 'move the glacial forces of the habitus into the quickened beat of improvisations for large groups of people' (Appadurai 1997: 6). He picks up on the work of the French theorist Michel de Certeau to argue that people are continuously confronted with images, narratives, information, voices and perspectives from all corners of the globe that don't equate with the received ideas of their habitus. Rather than having stable identities, people have to 'make do' with whatever is at hand, so to speak. So, for instance, regardless of their own national or ethnic identity, they might borrow identities from Hong Kong kung fu films, American sitcoms or Indian melodramas. This means that they are necessarily distanced not just from 'official' cultural texts and their meanings, but from any institution or text which claims to have a monopoly on meaning—simply because, in a globalised world, what is understood as normal is always subject to (very rapid) challenge and change. We will deal with this aspect of the habitus, and its relation to cultural fields, in our next chapter.

Conclusion

In this chapter we have looked at the three most important theoretical concepts developed by Bourdieu—cultural field, cultural capital and the habitus.
* Cultural field can be defined as a series of institutions, rules, rituals, conventions, categories, designations, appointments and titles which constitute an objective hierarchy, and which

produce and authorise certain discourses and activities. But it is also constituted by, or out of, the conflict which is involved when groups or individuals attempt to determine what constitutes capital within that field, and how that capital is to be distributed.

- Cultural capital acts as a social relation within a system of exchange, and the term is extended 'to all the goods, material and symbolic, without distinction, that present themselves as rare and worthy of being sought after in a particular social formation' (Harker et al. 1990: 1).
- Bourdieu refers to the partly unconscious 'taking in' of rules, values and dispositions as 'the habitus', which he defines as 'the durably installed generative principle of regulated improvisations . . . [which produces] practices' (1977a: 78). In other words, habitus can be understood as the values and dispositions gained from our cultural history that generally stay with us across contexts (they are durable and transposable). These values and dispositions allow us to respond to cultural rules and contexts in a variety of ways (because they allow for improvisations), but the responses are always largely determined—regulated—by where (and who) we have been in a culture.

Further reading

Bourdieu, Pierre 1990a, *In Other Words: Essays Towards a Reflexive Sociology*, Stanford University Press, Stanford

Bourdieu, Pierre 1990b, *The Logic of Practice*, Polity Press, Cambridge

Bourdieu, Pierre 1977a, *Outline of a Theory of Practice*, Cambridge University Press, Cambridge

3

Theorising practice

In Chapters 1 and 2 we described the contexts that influenced Bourdieu's work, and the main theoretical concepts—capital, field and habitus—that he uses in his research and writings. In this chapter we will consider how Bourdieu puts those 'theoretical technologies' to work in attempting to bridge the apparent divide between 'academic theories' and everyday practices. It is important to pay attention to this issue, because Bourdieu has insisted on the close relation between his theories and the specific contexts in which they are employed, and out of which they (in a sense) arose.

One of the important aspects of this (which we discuss in more detail in Chapter 4) is the question of methodology, which is clearly central both to sociology, the discipline in which Bourdieu predominantly works, and to cognate disciplines into which he crosses—such as anthropology, cultural studies, communication studies, politics, literary studies, history and ethnography. The main issue at stake is the:

> considerable hostility between what is seen as the methodological–quantitative side of the field and the theoretical– qualitative side. Moreover, practitioners of one or another specialty tend to inhabit different intellectual networks, and hence to condemn each other's position *in absentia*, without knowing much about it. (Randall Collins, quoted in Bourdieu 1992d: 32)

Bourdieu makes considerable use of quantitative analysis, but he is wary of, and clearly reacts against, the instrumental positivism which, as far as social research and analysis in the United States is concerned, has 'ruled virtually unchallenged since the 1940s' (1992d: 31). One of the problems with positivism, for Bourdieu, is the extent to which it has functioned as an instrument for what Foucault would call the regulation of populations. In other words, quasi-scientific disciplines (such as behavioural psychology, criminology and sociology) have been picked up and deployed by social institutions (including courts, prisons, police, welfare institutions and corporations). We find them used as a means of making judgments about the normality, health, sanity, employability, reliability, or guilt of individuals; and also to provide more generalised snapshots of class relations, social trends, consumer patterns, racial attitudes and gender proclivities. The point is that because this type of quantitative research tends to lack a theoretical or reflexive dimension, the knowledge these disciplines produce is invariably 'reproductive'. That is to say, it simply reproduces—rather than tests—the knowledge systems on which the research is based.

Because of this reproductive tendency, instrumental positivism is usually, though not exclusively, associated with the maintenance of social and cultural power relations. A discipline might quantitatively 'prove', for instance, that criminality or violence has a basis in racial identities. But it can only do this by presuming the notions of criminality or violence, and then by editing out a variety of contexts and factors (poverty, a lack of educational capital, demographics) that might predispose groups to certain types of behaviour. Bourdieu is scathing in his criticism of this kind of professional instrumentalism:

> As long as you take it as it presents itself, the given (the hallowed *data* of positivist sociologists) gives itself to you without difficulty. Everything goes smoothly, everything is taken for granted. Doors and mouths open wide. What group would turn down the sacralizing and naturalizing recording of the social scientist? . . . In short, as long as you remain within the realm of socially sanctioned appearances—and

this is the order to which the notion of 'profession' belongs—
you will have all appearances with you and for you, even the
appearance of scientificity. (1992d: 244)

So Bourdieu is, as we see here, deeply opposed to the untheorised
use of data. He also refuses to fetishise theory for theory's sake,
and although he is recognised as a major social theorist, and
his theoretical terminology (terms like habitus, cultural capital,
distinction) is being used in an increasing number of fields and
disciplines, he rejects the notion that he is a 'theorist'. Questioned
by an interviewer as to whether 'there is a theory *in* your work,
or to be more precise, a set of "thinking tools" . . . of wide—if not
universal—applicability', Bourdieu agrees, but with the following qualification:

> these tools are only visible through the results they yield, and
> they are not built as such. The ground for these tools . . . lies
> in research, in the practical problems and puzzles encountered
> and generated in the effort to construct a phenomenally
> diverse set of objects in such a way that they can be treated,
> thought of, comparatively. (1992d: 160)

An important distinction is being made here between theory as
a kind of language game almost exclusively involved in and for
itself, and theory as something (a 'tool') that enables you to understand and deal with problems and difficulties. Bourdieu's
theories are produced by, and always oriented towards, a task—
for instance, making sense of why students from different class
positions have different success rates at school. This practical
dimension to his theorising is diametrically opposed to what he
calls the 'scholastic point of view', which he defines as:

> a very peculiar point of view on the social world, on language,
> on any possible object of thought that is made possible by the
> situation of . . . leisure, of which the school . . . is a particular
> form, as an institutionalized situation of studious leisure.
> Adoption of this scholastic point of view is the admission fee
> tacitly demanded by all scholarly fields: the neutralizing
> disposition (in Husserl's sense), implying the bracketing of all
> theses of existence and all practical intentions. (1998d: 127–8)

Quantitative and qualitative analysis

Bourdieu's work is based on an attempt to think through the divide between quantitative and qualitative positions. His logic of research is 'inseparably empirical and theoretical' (1992d: 160), and he argues that 'one cannot think well except in and through theoretically constructed empirical cases' (1992d: 160). This has ramifications for the ways in which Bourdieu's work (and in particular his theories) can be picked up and used by researchers. There are two main questions that need to be addressed. First, Bourdieu argues that his theoretical notions are tied closely to empirical cases: but what does he mean by 'empirical cases'? And second, is the validity of a theory limited to specific cases?

Let us take the second question first. A theoretical notion is generally applicable, according to Bourdieu, only in the sense that it arises out of 'an historical analysis of the specific properties of contemporary societies' (1992d: 159). We can accept that the notion of cultural capital might have been derived from the inter-section of a particular social issue (say, the academic performance of students in schools) and the methodologies used to bring this issue to light in an empirical way (say, the formulation of questionnaires and surveys). But what also has to be factored in are the other discourses, accounts, observations, testimonies, documents, examples and personal experiences or knowledge that testify (in the researcher's professional opinion) to both the historical and contemporary validity of the notion of cultural capital.

To return, now, to the first question: what Bourdieu refers to as 'empirical cases' are always much more than themselves. After all, Bourdieu could not even begin to identify what constituted the object of an empirical study (say, the academic performance of students in schools) without bringing various literacies and forms of knowledge (quantitative and otherwise) into play (for instance, what will be included as a 'school'; what do we understand by 'academic performance', and so on). So in order both to construct an empirical object of study, and ensure its general validity, empiricism must be (and is) mediated by qualitative factors (such as historical accounts). Later in this chapter we will look specifically, through reference to *The Weight of the World*, at the ways in which Bourdieu attempts to 'contextualise' his empirical research through the use of rigorous 'self-reflexive' techniques taken, appropriately enough, from his own theories of field and habitus.

Reflexivity and epistemology

It is clear that for Bourdieu theoretical notions (such as habitus or cultural capital) aren't simply theoretical filters which process social practices; rather, they are technologies which are transformed, and need to be rethought, as they are applied. How generally applicable are Bourdieu's theories? They are so to the extent to which they can be used as temporary constructs to provide evidence for, and demonstrate the specific properties of, social groups and practices. But how is it possible for Bourdieu to come to an understanding of the forces and influences that inform and drive the various relationships, ideas, meanings and practices that constitute society? After all, Bourdieu's own work—and in particular his notion of the relationship between practice and the habitus—would seem to limit the extent to which agents can come to know and understand their own specific contexts and motives.

For Bourdieu, the extent to which agents can attain knowledge of, and negotiate, various cultural fields is dependent on, and can be explained in terms of, two epistemological types. The first he terms a 'practical sense' or a 'logic of practice', while the second involves a 'reflexive' relation to cultural fields and one's own practices within those fields.

Bourdieu characterises practical sense as an ability to comprehend and negotiate cultural fields; and to explain this more fully, he compares it to a sportsperson's

> feel for the game. Having the feel for the game is . . . to master in a practical way the future of the game, is to have a sense of the history of the game. While the bad player is off tempo, always too early or too late, the good player is the one who anticipates, who is ahead of the game. (1998d: 80)

What Bourdieu is referring to here is knowing the game that is played out between agents in cultural fields, which involves a knowledge of the various rules (written and unwritten), genres, discourses, forms of capital, values and imperatives which inform and determine agents' practices, and which are continuously being transformed by those agents and their practices. This knowledge allows agents to make sense of what is happening around them, and to make strategic decisions as to how a field or fields should be negotiated—in other words, which practices, genres or discourses are appropriate in certain circumstances. When a person invites someone they are romantically interested in back home for a massage, or an office worker decides to enrol in a university degree, or a journalist interviews a politician, they are all playing a game with potentially positive and negative consequences (romance or loneliness; promotion or stagnation; a big story or a non-event), depending on the appropriateness of the decisions they make (Is inviting someone back for a massage too forward? Is there enough time to work and study successfully? Will the politician 'spill the beans' under aggressive questioning?).

The second epistemological type constitutes an extension of the practical sense, which is, for Bourdieu, quite restricted, because a field more or less 'speaks us'. That is, we naturalise, embody and act out the imperatives, values and dispositions of the field in which we are operating. (Imagine, say, a football player who refused to be competitive, or who apologised every time he bumped into—or tackled—another player. Even if this football player were normally diffident and polite, in order to be successful on the field he would 'naturally' perform in a more assertive manner.) In order to overcome (at least partly) the limitations under which we operate within a particular field, Bourdieu posits the need for a 'reflexive' relation to our own practices, with particular regard to three main aspects or contexts. The first of these is our social and cultural origins and categories (say, generation, class, religion, ethnicity); the second is our position in whatever field we are located (as an anthropologist, journalist or bureaucrat, for example); and the third is what Bourdieu refers to as an 'intellectual bias', that is, a tendency for some agents (in fields such as the arts and academe) to 'abstract' practices, and to see them as ideas to be contemplated, rather than problems to be solved.

The distinction between practical knowledge and a more reflexive sense or understanding can be appreciated if we take a couple of examples from the sport—and field— of football (what Australians and Americans call 'soccer'). Once a player is on the pitch, what they do, the decisions they take and the moves they make are all based on a certain 'practical literacy' with regard to the laws, rules, values, abilities and tactics 'of the field'. In a World Cup game in France in 1998 involving England and Argentina, an Argentinian player fouled England's David Beckham, knocking him to the ground. As the referee came in to admonish the Argentinian, Beckham, thinking that the referee was distracted, instinctively but very deliberately kicked the Argentinian. Unfortunately the referee saw what happened; and his view of the incident—and its gravity—was enhanced by the reaction of the Argentinian, who immediately (again, instinctively but deliberately) reacted as if mortally wounded. Both these actions were 'of the moment', examples of the two players trying to get the better of the other by exploiting their 'practical sense' (Beckham believed the referee would be distracted and the Argentinian an easy target; the Argentinian was going to make sure the referee sent Beckham off—which he did).

If we stay with the world of football we can get an idea of how a more reflexive knowledge manifests itself. The former Manchester United footballer (now film star) Eric Cantona was famous for giving quirky or 'difficult' interviews: he never said the expected things ('We gave our best', 'We're taking it one day at a time'), but tended instead to 'play' with journalists. When asked at a post-match conference if he was surprised at the large number of journalists in attendance, all waiting on his every word, he said something like, 'When the seagulls follow the fishing trawler, it is because they expect to catch a few discarded fish'. Now this caused a sensation, not because anyone understood what he was talking about (they clearly didn't), but because the journalists had got what they wanted—an example of Cantona being quirky and mysterious and 'philosophical'. This, of course, was exactly the point Cantona was making: he knew the journalists and what they wanted (more evidence of his Gallic eccentricity), so he gave them a 'story' about a trawler (Cantona) being followed by seagulls (journalists) hoping to catch a few discarded fish (eccentric quotes).

Some critics have accused Bourdieu of confining this reflexivity to the field of sociology. In fact, Bourdieu associates the capacity for reflexivity (and the epistemological advantages it potentially provides) with a variety of positions, fields and groups, including literature (1992d: 206–8), science (1992d: 175–6) and art (1995: 1). Reflexivity is not, for Bourdieu, the product of one privileged field, but rather can characterise any field which allows for, or disposes its agents towards, 'the systematic exploration of the unthought categories of thought which delimit the thinkable and predetermine the thought' (1992d: 40).

This notion of reflexivity informs Bourdieu's work in three main ways. First, it more or less defines what he calls 'science' or scientific inquiry in terms of the notion of a radical doubt. Second, and relatedly, it contextualises social issues and objects of knowledge within a historical framework. Third, it requires that all scientific or research activity be understood in terms of an ethical imperative.

Bourdieu makes the point that research activity often tends to take as given the values, questions and categories of the field and the society in which it operates. Reflexivity produces a break with this mindset through reference to the notion of radical doubt as a departure point for any research activity. As Bourdieu writes:

> The construction of a scientific object requires first and foremost a break with common sense, that is, with the representations shared by all . . . *The preconstructed is everywhere.* The sociologist is literally beleaguered by it, as everyone else is. The sociologist is thus saddled with the task of knowing an object—the social world—of which he is the product, in a way such that the problems that he raises about it and the concepts he uses have every chance of being the product of this object itself. (1992d: 235)

In other words, what might seem to be a compelling research problem worthy of great study can turn out to be an abstraction created by the field of sociology itself, geared towards serving the interests of that field and its agents rather than the outside world. So while research into the experience of an underclass in the streets of Bangkok might seem really valuable, the problem is that the category of the underclass is already preconstructed within the field of sociology. This means that the sociologist risks fitting the experience of people into a conceptual frame which has no meaning to them and which only makes sense within the play of interests in the sociological field. The research outcomes from such a study would only confirm the sociologist's removal from the outside world.

We made the point in Chapter 1 that Bourdieu's theories and approaches owed a great deal to a (largely unacknowledged) Nietzschean legacy. Nowhere is this more apparent than the way in which Nietzsche's notion of genealogy is taken up by Bourdieu as one of the means of overcoming the tendency for researchers to reproduce 'common sense' in one form or another. The various values, discourses, traditions and rituals that characterise a field, and present themselves as if they have always characterised that field, have a history. Now for Bourdieu (as for Nietzsche) the task of scientific inquiry is to investigate the politics of what we can call the 'imposition of common sense'. Most researchers have a vested interest in not subjecting their own positions and approaches to historical inquiry. Bourdieu responded to a question about the place of history in his thinking in the following way:

> Suffice it to say that *the separation of sociology and history is a disastrous division,* and one totally devoid of epistemological justification: all sociology should be historical and all history sociological. In point of fact, one of the functions of the theory of fields that I propose is to make the opposition between reproduction and transformation, statics and dynamics, or structure and history, vanish . . . [W]e cannot grasp the dynamics of a field . . . without a historical, that is, a genetic, analysis of its constitution and of the tensions that exist between positions in it, as well as between this field and other fields, and especially the field of power. (1992d: 90)

The combination of radical doubt and genealogical analysis provide the means—a scientific method—by which researchers can investigate and uncover not only the specific properties of a society, and the ways that those properties came about and were naturalised, but also who benefits and who loses from such processes. In other words, Bourdieu equates reflexive science with an epistemological ethics which is very close to the position Foucault articulates in his essay 'What is Enlightenment'. For Foucault, the Enlightenment provided scholars with 'an attitude, an ethos . . . in which the critique of what we are is at one and the same time the historical analysis of the limits imposed on us and the experiment with the possibility of going beyond them' (Foucault 1997: 319). For Bourdieu, scientific reflexivity performs a similar function because it provides the possibility of an awakening of consciousness. He writes:

> I believe that when sociology remains at a highly abstract and formal level, it contributes nothing. When it gets down to the nitty gritty of real life, however, it is an instrument that people can apply to themselves for quasi-clinical purposes. The true freedom that sociology offers is to give us a small chance of knowing what game we play and of minimizing the ways in which we are manipulated by the forces of the field in which we evolve . . . [Sociology] allows us to discern the sites where we do indeed enjoy a degree of freedom and those where we do not. (1992d: 198–9)

Reflexivity and social practice

How does Bourdieu's scientific reflexivity inform his research into social practices? The extent to which Bourdieu is committed to combining theoretical reflexivity with empirical rigour is perhaps best demonstrated in his book *The Weight of the World*. Under his direction, a team of researchers spent three years interviewing predominantly lower-class men and women in France about the conditions of their everyday lives. The interviews were then transcribed and written up more or less as a series of short stories. The main point of the book was to come to an understanding of the conditions and factors which produced the 'pain and misery' of everyday life; but Bourdieu also attempted, in this project, to communicate 'the simultaneously practical and theoretical problems that emerge from the particular interaction between the interviewer and the person being questioned' (1999a: 607).

The Weight of the World constitutes Bourdieu's most ambitious attempt to go beyond the problems associated with positivism, such as the way in which the types of questions posed by the interviewer and the situation of the interview itself (location, time, differences of understanding) work to 'construct', rather than elicit, the responses of those interviewed. He does this by way of a particularly rigorous commitment, affecting virtually all aspects of the project, to transforming empirical research into a self-reflexive science.

How does Bourdieu go about this in *The Weight of the World*? In a postscript to the book entitled, appropriately, 'Understanding', he identifies five main areas which help produce self-reflexive research, and which he employs in the book and the research:

- First, there is a need to make explicit the project's intentions and procedural principles, so that readers can make sense of what is happening, and why.
- Second, there is a need to clarify what interviewees can and cannot say, and the contexts which work to 'censor' their responses.
- Third, there is the problem of overcoming the limitations of transcription, which invariably 'edits out' much of the sense of what an interviewee is communicating (by not taking into account irony, or body language). Bourdieu suggests that the answer 'lies in the permanent control of the point of view, which is continually affirmed in the details of the writing (the fact . . . of saying "her school" not "the school", in order to signal the fact that the account of what happens . . . is given by the teacher interviewed and not the analyst)' (1999a: 625).
- Fourth, it is essential that interviewers have an extensive knowledge of the social contexts of their subjects, both

through general research and as a result of having a 'history' of interviewing the same interviewee.

- Fifth, the interviewers also need to objectify their own social position, and try to 'forget it'; that is, they need to free themselves, as far as is possible, from preconceived notions and values taken from their own habitus.

What are supposed to be the main effects of this methodological self-reflexivity? According to Bourdieu, the care and rigour that is evident in the interviewing process allows the researchers to be more sympathetic and empathic interviewers, and this, along with offering the interviewees an 'absolutely exceptional situation for communication, free from the usual constraints (particularly of time)' (1999a: 614), enables the interviewees to 'grasp this situation as an exceptional opportunity offered to them to testify, to make themselves heard, to carry their experience over from the private to the public sphere' (1999a: 615). The transformation of this private testimony into public knowledge corresponds to what Bourdieu understands as the ethical and political imperative that drives his work:

> Producing awareness of the mechanisms that make life painful, even unlivable, does not neutralize them; bringing contradictions to light does not resolve them. But, as skeptical as one may be about the efficacy of the sociological message, one has to acknowledge the effect it can have in allowing those who suffer to find out that their suffering can be imputed to social causes and thus to feel exonerated; and in making generally known the social origin, collectively hidden, of unhappiness in all its forms, including the most intimate, the most secret. (1999a: 629)

Reflexivity, cultural field and habitus

Up to this point we have described the ways in which Bourdieu has theorised about, and used those theories and related approaches to research, cultural practices. But if, following Bourdieu, we accept that no cultural practice is explicable without reference to cultural field and habitus, then the same must be true of Bourdieu's theories of practice. To what extent are Bourdieu's theories of practice explicable with regard to, or in terms of, the field(s) in which he works? In order to consider this issue, we will look at Michel de Certeau's description and analysis of Bourdieu's work and theories as 'strategic moves' in a kind of scholarly game.

Certeau demonstrates how closely Bourdieu's work is attuned to specific instances or moments of practice. This constitutes a reversal of the usual sociological value of understanding practices in terms of generalised rules and conventions which remain the same regardless of the context. He identifies a variety of strategies—moves in a game—that emerge from Bourdieu's analysis of the ongoing relation between people, social rules and conventions, and specific times and places—what we could call 'cultural literacy' (Schirato & Yell 2000). This expression picks up on three aspects of strategic thinking that are essential to the success of any practice:

- First, there needs to be a self-reflexive understanding of the person's own position and resources within the field(s) or institution(s) in which they are operating.
- Second, there should be an awareness of the rules, regulations, values and cultural capital (both official and unofficial) which characterise the field of activity.
- Third, and most importantly, what is required is an ability to manoeuvre as best as possible, given the handicaps associated with, for instance, a lack of cultural capital, within the situations and conditions which consist of such aspects as how realisable a goal or desire is, what capital is held by competing persons, and what opportunities exist to turn a particular rule to one's advantage.

The identification and demonstration of these three key elements of cultural literacy—self-reflexivity, an understanding of social rules and regulations, and an ability to negotiate conditions and contexts 'of the moment'—is one of the major achievements of Bourdieu's theorising of practice. His willingness to allow that people are capable of responding to, and altering, their activities in the face of complex and variable conditions means that he can follow their practices and procedures because he remains (theoretically) open to all possibilities, regardless of whether they are found in social rules or sociological knowledge. Certeau contends, however, that Bourdieu's own attempts to account for practices are themselves sometimes delimited by the 'prison-house' of the habitus.

As we pointed out in Chapter 2, habitus is the way Bourdieu moves between objectivism and subjectivism. Practices cannot be understood simply in terms of the narratives, rules, values, discourses and ideologies of a field (that is, objectivity), nor in terms of individual, uncontextualised decision making (that is, subjectivity). Rather a person acquires a habitus, which strongly influences all subsequent actions and beliefs. The habitus is made up of a number of ways of operating, and inclinations, values and rationales that are acquired from various formative contexts, such as the family, the education system, or class contexts.

Bourdieu insists, however, that practices, and the negotiations, deliberations and option-takings that produce them, are simultaneously conscious and unconscious. In other words, people do think and act in strategic ways, and try to use the rules of the game to their advantage, but at the same time they are influenced—or almost driven—by the values and expectations that they get from the habitus. So though they may be conscious of making moves and acting strategically, they are unaware that their motives, goals and aspirations are not spontaneous or natural, but are given to them through the habitus.

Certeau uses Bourdieu's work on the relationship between habitus and practice in order to demonstrate that the position Bourdieu arrives at in a text such as *Outline of a Theory of Practice*— which is, effectively, that habitus always drives practice—is contradicted by his own insights. Bourdieu argues that the Kabylians (an Algerian people, one of two groups—the other being the people of the Béarnaise region of France—that Bourdieu studies, describes and analyses in *Outline*) are both inventive and strategic in the way they inhabit their society, but their goals always correspond to the logic of their habitus, whereas for Certeau they:

> 'navigate' among the rules, 'play with all the possibilities offered by traditions', make use of one tradition rather than another, compensate for one by means of another. Taking advantage of the flexible surface which covers up the hard core, they create their own relevance in this network.
> (Certeau 1984: 54)

And he goes on to point out the burden that Bourdieu, in the absence of any possibility of a self-conscious, dynamic cultural literacy, asks habitus to carry. His habitus-driven explanation of Kabylian practices means there is:

> no choice among several possibilities, and thus no 'strategic intention'; there is no introduction of correctives due to better information, and thus not 'the slightest calculation'; there is no prediction, but only an 'assumed world' as the repetition of the past. In short, 'it is because subjects do not know, strictly speaking, what they are doing, that what they do has more meaning than they realize' . . . a cleverness that does not recognise itself as such. (Certeau 1984: 56)

A good example of this issue is the way players operate and function on the sporting field. Soccer players, for instance, are familiar with all the rules, both written (offside, no outfielder can use a hand to control the ball) and unwritten (if one team kicks the ball out of play to stop the game when a player gets injured, the other team is 'obliged' to throw it back to them when play resumes). They are also aware of various circumstances that influence or determine how a referee will enforce the rules, or which rules will be emphasised or ignored (a home team is more likely to be awarded penalties; referees might have received a directive to stamp out tackles from behind, but will go easy on minor offences). Both Bourdieu and Certeau would agree that players take all these contexts and circumstances into account on the field. Players from the home side, knowing that the referee is being influenced by the home crowd, might be inclined to 'dive' (that is, fall over) in the penalty area at the slightest touch from an opposing player. Players from the away side know this, and will go out of their way to avoid any kind of contact. In other words, a game is going on within the game which has nothing to do with the rules of the game, and players have to use their cultural literacies to negotiate a context which is never officially articulated. The habitus of the players incorporates these fluctuations (that is, rules are codified, but they are always changing) and contradictions (that is, the game is never what it officially says it is), and allows the players to respond practically and appropriately.

Where Bourdieu and Certeau would part company on this issue is with regard to the extent to which players can move outside their habitus. Bourdieu's point would be that if the referee awarded an unjust penalty (say, because of crowd pressure), the team that benefited might react in a number of ways (unabashed joy, subdued celebrations), but they could never react in a way that was outside the habitus—say, by foregoing the penalty, deliberately kicking the ball wide of the posts, appealing to the crowd to be fair and equitable in their barracking, or admonishing the player who had 'dived'. For Bourdieu, the habitus of the players (strongly informed by a competitive ethos) would render such behaviour unthinkable. Certeau, on the other hand, would argue that such behaviour was inarticulable rather than unthinkable; that is, the penalty taker could ensure justice was done (and move beyond the constraints of the habitus) by deliberately missing the penalty without letting anyone know what was really happening. Bourdieu might reply that this was simply a case of one aspect of the player's habitus (for instance the player might be deeply religious) 'kicking in' to override other dispositions (competitiveness or team interest). But Certeau's point is that Bourdieu (or anybody else, for that matter) can never really know a practice, and in this he is backed up by Bourdieu's own statement that resistance 'takes the most unexpected forms, to the point of remaining more or less invisible to the cultivated eye' (1990a: 155).

Certeau argues that Bourdieu's refusal to give serious consideration to what his own analysis clearly demonstrates (that is, the Kabylia know what they are doing) is a form of tactic: after all, Bourdieu is operating within the field of sociology, a science that expects its practitioners to be able to produce scientific 'truths' and deliver certainties—which is, in a sense, a role the notion of the habitus plays in Bourdieu's work. In our next chapter we will look, in detail, at the extent to which Bourdieu's work is influenced by, and attempts to negotiate, the field of sociology, as well as related fields such as anthropology and ethnography.

Conclusion

- Bourdieu has insisted on the close relation between his theories and the specific contexts in which they are employed, and out of which they (in a sense) arose.
- Bourdieu's work is based on an attempt to think through the divide between quantitative and qualitative positions. His logic of research is 'inseparably empirical and theoretical' (1992d: 160), and he argues that 'one cannot think well except in and through theoretically constructed empirical cases' (1992d: 160).
- For Bourdieu, the extent to which agents can attain knowledge of, and negotiate, various cultural fields is dependent on, and can be explained in terms of, two epistemological types. The first he terms a 'practical sense' or a 'logic of practice', while the second involves a 'reflexive' relation to cultural fields and one's own practices within those fields.
- Bourdieu's willingness to allow that people are capable of responding to, and altering, their activities in the face of complex and variable conditions means that he can follow their practices and procedures because he remains open to all possibilities, regardless of whether they are found in social rules or sociological knowledge. Michel de Certeau contends, however, that Bourdieu's own attempts to account for practices are themselves sometimes delimited by the 'prison-house' of the habitus.

Further reading

Bourdieu, Pierre and Loïc Wacquant 1992d, *An Invitation to Reflexive Sociology*, Polity Press, Cambridge

Bourdieu, Pierre 1998d, *Practical Reason*, Polity Press, Cambridge

Bourdieu, Pierre et al. 1999, *The Weight of the World: Social Suffering in Contemporary Society*, Stanford University Press, Stanford

Certeau, Michel de 1984, *The Practice of Everyday Life*, University of California Press, Berkeley

Schirato, Tony and Susan Yell 2000, *Communication and Cultural Literacy*, 2nd edn, Allen & Unwin/Sage, Sydney and London

4

Bourdieu's sociology

Bourdieu's official title is Professor of Sociology, but the sociology he does is somewhat different from that practised in most English-speaking countries. In the United Kingdom, the United States and Australia, for instance, sociology is typically defined most simply as 'the study of people in groups'. Bourdieu argues that this is too limiting—that sociology emerged out of 'an initial error of definition' which split the social sciences up into those that look at individuals and those that look at collectives, without understanding that individuals exist only alongside and within collective structures, and so cannot be understood in isolation from one other (see *Sociology in Question* 1993b: 15).

Bourdieu also differs somewhat from British, Australian or American sociologists because many of them base their work on the writings of sociology's 'founding fathers'—especially Weber, Durkheim and Marx—and stake its status as a 'science' on the extensive use of statistics, and methodological rigour. Bourdieu identifies a wider field open to him in his work, and sees no need to locate himself within one or other sociological lineage. In fact, when asked why he reads various authors, he replied 'You get what you can where you can' (1990a: 29). He writes in the opening pages of his textbook, *The Craft of Sociology* (1991c), that it is not particularly important to identify whether a piece of sociological work can be affiliated with a particular 'school' of sociology. This is not to suggest that he neglects major sociologists. As he writes in *In Other Words*, 'Authors—Marx, Durkheim, Weber, and so on—represent landmarks which structure our theoretical space and our perception of this space' (1990a: 30), and he goes on in this and other books to show precisely how these authors have been landmarks for him. He particularly acknowledges his debt to these three 'fathers' in the work each produced to show the importance, for sociologists, of breaking with 'naive realism' and 'moralizing naivete' (1991c: 33, 40), and deploying rigorous research methods and logic. Still, more than many other sociologists, he clearly relies more on philosophical approaches than on the 'grand theorists' when making sense of social groups and social practice.

Not surprisingly, many sociologists regard Bourdieu's work as incurably theoretical and 'philosophical'; but, ironically, many philosophers and cultural theorists see him as too committed to empiricism. In fact, as we discussed in Chapter 3, he is cautiously committed to both, and criticises the way in which his own writings are often taken as 'grand theory': 'I blame most of my readers for having considered as theoretical treatises . . . works that, like gymnastics handbooks, were intended for exercise, or even better, for being put into practice' ('Concluding remarks', in Calhoun et al. 1993a: 271).

His approach to research methods is rather different from 'traditional' sociological approaches. Although like other sociologists Bourdieu uses empirical methodologies, including statistics, surveys, questionnaires and interviews—whether examining art (in *Distinction* or *The Love of Art*), social stratification (in *The Weight of the World*), gender relations (*Masculine Domination*) or education (*Homo Academicus* or *State Nobility*)—he argues that he is more cautious about their value than are many other sociologists. Certainly he tends to analyse his findings from a philosophical and political perspective rather than rely on strictly quantitative analyses. He is not alone in this approach now; but arguably he was one of the first sociologists to take this tack, and to find ways of using sociological techniques that were both more philosophical and more rigorous. For instance, he has insisted from the very early days of his professional research work, when he was in Algeria and teaching sociology to potential statisticians at the *Ecole nationale de la statistique et des etudes economiques*, that it is not enough to collect and process data. Researchers must also understand the relationship between the object of study and the research methods applied to it. This is, he argues, because statistical data do not provide any access to 'facts'; their value is in the extent to which they can verify sociological ideas and findings.

He extends this attitude to all research methods, arguing that researchers must not rely on the strength of a research tool, but should think through the validity of each technique for each particular case. And, for Bourdieu, there are no all-purpose research tools, so teaching students how to use such tools or methodologies while not providing adequate training in epistemologies or the philosophy of science can, he suggests, lead to research errors. Indeed, a fascination with, or fetishising of, methodological instruments can lead to the failure to critique the methods themselves. As he argues, too much attention to instruments is 'liable to make researchers forget that, in order to observe certain facts, they should not so much refine the observing and measuring instruments as question the routine use that is made of the instruments' (1991c: 62).

While his sort of caution about trust in methodologies or statistics is found in many current textbooks on social research methods, Bourdieu is still, arguably, one of the most vocal sociologists in arguing that researchers must understand epistemology (that is, theories of knowledge) and construction (the notion that objects of research exist, for researchers, only within the framework of their hypothesis). 'The fundamental scientific act', he writes, 'is the construction of the object; you don't move to the real without a hypothesis, without instruments of construction' (1991c: 248). And he insists that researchers should constantly take into account their own presuppositions about their field of research, and understand the extent to which their way of seeing informs what they are likely to see, even if they do use rigorous statistical methods. This means that Bourdieu sees sociology as an applied, rather than a pure science. It is, he writes:

a critical science, critical of itself and the other sciences and also critical of the powers that be, including the powers of science. It's a science that strives to understand the laws of production of science . . . Sociology as I conceive it consists in transforming metaphysical problems into problems that can be treated scientifically and therefore politically. (1993b: 28)

In other words, for Bourdieu the point of sociology is not to gather information about how society is organised, but to critique the discourses and practices that stand for us as 'truths'. He sees sociology as dealing with a philosophical and a political, rather than a scientific, problem. This doesn't mean that he looks to sociology as the magic bullet that will save society from itself—what Georg Simmel called 'the magical word that would offer a solution to all the riddles of history and practical life' (Simmel, 1998: 283). What he says, rather, is that a rigorous social analysis makes it more difficult for authoritarian or totalitarian forms of social organisation to come into power—and, as we describe in Chapter 10, his own work is actively involved in challenging such forms.

What Bourdieu 'does' as a sociologist is to look at the whole social world, and investigate how it is put together, and for whom it works. And what he seeks to answer in his sociological research are the following questions: how do we identify social 'calls to order'? what are the conditions for hearing such calls? and, which social groups and individuals are more inclined to respond to calls to order?

So, for Bourdieu, sociology first allows researchers to objectify themselves and their social worlds in order to break with everyday notions about how the world works; and second, it allows us to understand the extent to which social organisations are built on arbitrary divisions that serve particular interests. This is what he calls 'the struggle for the monopoly of the legitimate representation of the social world' (1990a: 180). And if we want to make sense of human practices, he suggests, we first need to make sense of the field(s) in which they are played out. At its best, sociology allows us to objectify the field and the game so that we can make sense of it, with as little bias or 'interest' as possible. It is a useful and potentially powerful discipline for this work because it maps out the historical and contextual grounds on which the present social order is based, and by doing this 'denaturalises' the social world, showing that it is arbitrary (not based on an inherent necessity) and contingent (of the moment, rather than permanent and immutable), rather than inevitable or natural.

In Chapter 2 we discussed how Bourdieu uses the concept of field; and sociology itself can be understood as a field in these terms because, if we are to make sense of what it is and how it works, we need to be familiar with the contexts in which it emerged as a 'science', the contexts in which it is operating now, and the sorts of things that are at stake in any social research. And we have to understand that we bring our own prejudices (our personal history, or habitus), and our own background (including our class, race and gender) to the social research process, to our selection of tools of social research, and hence to the 'spectacles' through which we look at the social problem we intend to investigate.

Another issue that affects how sociologists may approach their work is that they are members of a community of sociologists all competing for research resources, cultural capital and claims to authority, validity and authenticity. And while competing with one another, they are also competing with other forms of social science (psychology, anthropology, even economics). At the same time, they have to take into account the varying claims of personal interest, the demands of the institution that is paying for the research and so on. And there is also the effect of what Bourdieu terms 'the intellectualist bias' which can be found in academic settings, and which can lead researchers to take up research projects principally because they are academically interesting and not because they are a 'real' social problem; or because they offer an opportunity to examine the field without necessarily having really to understand the logic of practice in that field. All this threatens research objectivity.

This is not to say that sociology is a flawed science—or no more flawed than any other science, anyway. For Bourdieu, what is absolutely critical in any scientific research is that the theoretical model deployed must be able to 'see through' the situation—break with appearances—and be generalisable so that it can be applied to similar conditions and contexts. But it is also important not to see the concept of 'field' as anything other than a methodological tool, and one that should always be open to critique. He writes, 'The operations of practice are only as good as the theory in which they are grounded, because theory owes its position in the hierarchy of operations to the fact that it actualizes the epistemological primacy of reason over experience' (1991c: 63).

Some writers have critiqued Bourdieu's emphasis on field, and suggested that his approach can easily slide into the sorts of problems he warns against. They suggest, that is, that his idea that field is the best or only way of objectifying a social situation can lead researchers into a paint-by-numbers approach, so that once the positions, values and discourses of the field have been identified, the researchers think they know everything that needs to be known about that social problem. These objections should be taken seriously, but researchers need to bear in mind that Bourdieu's field is not a real or concrete space: it is a metaphor for a social site where people and institutions engage in particular activities. His field exists only relationally, only as a set of possibilities, or a series of moves; as the site of particular forms of capital and particular narratives; and, especially, as the site of regulatory and coercive discourses.

These attitudes shape Bourdieu's approach to sociology and social research in several ways. First, it means that he has had to develop and deploy what he calls 'a reflexive sociology'. This means that researchers must always check their personal presumptions, take into account their personal circumstances, and in other ways actively correct the sorts of biases that sneak into even the most carefully crafted piece of social research. As he shows, theory is a 'principle of vision and division' (1990a: 18), so even the best theorised sociological program can never be innocent or uncontaminated by interest. But if sociologists keep this in mind, they are more likely to produce work that at best minimises its bias, and at least alerts readers to the sorts of conditions in which it was undertaken. This emphasis on self-reflexivity does not, though, mean that Bourdieu claims to have achieved a state of 'disinterest'—or even that such a state is desirable. While, like other sociologists, he warns against bias and interest, he also points out that the researcher's possible 'interest' should not be simply put aside in favour of indifference because 'Indifference,' he writes, 'is . . . a state of knowledge in which I am not capable of differentiating the stakes proposed' (1992d: 116).

He has always been clear about the importance of 'differentiating the stakes proposed', and the extent to which his work is 'interested'. Indeed, as his co-researcher Loïc Wacquant reports, his career has been marked by political engagement: in the 1950s, when with others he resisted the censorship that was being imposed on their intellectual life at the *Ecole normale*; in 1960s Algeria, when he entered into the war zone itself to report on colonialist oppression of the Algerians by the French; and in 1968 when, with other intellectuals, he participated in the student uprisings. During the 1970s he continued to insist on progressive politics in the face of an increasingly conservative intellectual climate. In the 1980s and throughout the 1990s he has been a critic of the government, and has increasingly taken an active political role by reporting on television or in the other mass media on social and political issues, from local anti-racist protests to pressuring the government about its global responsibilities. At the same time, he suggests in *Masculine Domination* (2001: 109) that we not 'surrender to what Virginia Woolf called "the pleasure of disillusioning" (which is no doubt one of the satisfactions surreptitiously pursued by sociology)'. Though he is here writing particularly of the magical world of love, he is also making a general statement about the work of sociology, and its limits. Its function is not simply to critique society or make manifest the 'real state of things'; it is not capable of achieving, once and for all, a change to the social order; nor do we undertake sociological work simply to sort out the theoretical problem. Rather, it is 'an endless labour, endlessly recommenced' (2001: 110) by which researchers strive to understand and demonstrate the social, historical, economic and political conditions that lead to the establishment of structures of power, and struggles for symbolic power, in any field and across society. Armed with this sort of knowledge, researchers may seek to intervene in the social struggle, or offer opportunities for others to intervene. Interestingly, though, for a sociologist so committed to political struggle he warns most particularly against research predominantly driven by politics:

> one cannot overestimate the risks that arise from any scientific project that allows its object to be imposed on it by external considerations, however noble and generous they may be. 'Good causes' are no substitute for epistemological justifications. (2001: 113)

In other words, poor sociology, or a failure of reflexivity because of the researcher's own political leanings or bias, is unlikely to lead to good social politics. We will discuss later in this chapter the techniques he suggests for minimising bias while still retaining the sorts of 'ethical investment' that mark quality research.

Anthropological Algeria

Bourdieu began developing these sorts of political and research perspectives during his earliest work in Algeria between 1957 and 1961, the period of the Algerian struggle for independence from France. What was particularly engrossing for him in this project, as he records in *The Algerians* (1962), was the opportunity to study the effects of colonialism, especially the transition of a community from traditional to more contemporary forms of social organisation, and the subsequent development in such communities of a 'capitalist' habitus. Initially his interest seems to have been in working through and evaluating research techniques and analytical frameworks. But by 1961 he had become more concerned with the politics of social organisation in Algeria, and with helping the Algerians deal with the process of change in their country and in their lifestyle. 'I wanted to be useful in order to overcome my guilty conscience about being merely a participant observer in this appalling war', he writes:

> I could not be content with reading left-wing newspapers or signing petitions; I had to do something as a scientist . . . I have never accepted the separation between the theoretical construction of the object of research and the set of practical procedures without which there can be no real knowledge. (1986b: 39)

The research he was conducting in Algeria was initially a form of ethnology, a social science in which the researcher observes 'the natives'. His approach was influenced, as we noted above, by his training in philosophy, but incorporated some sociological techniques because he was doing statistical surveys to analyse the social and economic conditions of some of the tribal groups in Algeria. He records that his perspective was also influenced, initially, by structuralism and Marxism: structuralism because he (and many others) saw it as an approach which melded philosophy and the human sciences, and Marxism because it suited his perspective that the 'objective relations' which structure the social world are more influential than the 'agents' (individuals) who inhabit that social world (1990a: 8). At this stage in his career he can be categorised as an anthropologist, because he was relying on observation and measurement, rather than simply thinking through issues (as would a philosopher), or testing and rehearsing theories (as might a conventional sociologist). But while he can no longer be understood as a structuralist, a Marxist or an anthropologist, he points out that what he was researching in Algeria was at heart the same issue he has continued to research in various fields ever since: 'the idea that struggles for recognition are a fundamental dimension of social life and that what is at stake in them is an accumulation of a particular form of capital' (1990a: 22). And having begun this work in a different culture, he has been able to continue it and to hone it in his home nation. The French writer Michel de Certeau writes that:

> Our 'tactics' seem to be analyzable only indirectly, through another society: . . . They return to us from afar, as though a different space were required in which to make visible and elucidate the tactics marginalized by the Western form of rationality. (1984: 50)

71

That is to say, sometimes it is necessary to take one's research and philosophical view 'elsewhere', in order to defamiliarise it and reflect on our basic preconceptions, and this seems to be precisely what Bourdieu experienced. In his recent *Masculine Domination*, for example, he closely examines gender relations in Algeria before shifting his gaze to gender relations in Europe, arguing that 'this detour through an exotic tradition is indispensable in order to break the relationship of deceptive familiarity that binds us to our own tradition' (2001: 3). And this is not a new technique for him: as early as 1959 and 1960, when he moved back to France, he applied some of the same methodologies he had used in Algeria to research marriage strategies in his home region of Béarn.

The physical relocation back to Europe also marks a point of transition in his work because, as an effect of his work in Algeria, he departed from structuralism and also from ethnology and anthropology. Structuralism, he found, could not account for the ways in which the habitus is able to generate an infinite number of possible moves, thus allowing people to adapt to their changing world. There were too many '-ology' words (1990a: 6), he thought, and too many gaps in its objective logic to make it a satisfactory research position. He moved away from ethnology too, because it relied too much on the privileged position of the researcher relative to the subjects of research to make it a useful and ethical methodology. Sociology became more attractive than any of these other methods because he found that within this discipline he was free to raise 'unthinkable questions'.

Sociology as practice

One reason he finds sociology a more rigorous approach to social practice than ethnology or structuralism is that he sees it as both an art and a craft. It is an art in that it brings the unseen things in society, or the things that are disguised, to light. It is a craft in that it involves the skillful making of a product (the research activity and its outcomes). Above all, sociology for Bourdieu is practical rather than abstract, a methodology that examines and engages with the small everyday details of life as well as the big questions, and that is prepared to 'get its hands dirty'. It is a constant process of finding, creating or identifying problems—problems in society that are worth investigating (because they are general problems, or problems with political outcomes), and problems for the researcher in the construction of a research method, and of the theoretical underpinnings of that method.

The object or practice that sparks this attention may be very broad or very specific. Bourdieu suggests two examples of where sociology can be used to explore a practice and expose a social problem. He reports, in *Distinction* and then again in *Field*, that he looked at art and investigated the relationship between its discourses and how working-class people actually use—or do not use—its products (music, galleries, photography). We discuss this work in more detail in Chapters 8 and 9. The second example comes from his reading of Erwin Panofsky (in 'Men and machines'). He records that Panofsky wondered why men raise their hats as a form of greeting, and found that it was a hangover from the Middle Ages practice, among knights, of raising their helmets to signal that their intentions were peaceful. Panofsky used his research into this 'problem', and the knowledge of the origin of the practice, to point to the importance of history in shaping bodily practice. In Bourdieu's first example, a set of discourses and a set of principles of vision and division that apparently pertain only to the artistic field can be seen to have a more general effect in shaping how working-class people under-stand their relationship to 'culture' and to particular cultural products. In his second example, a very small and apparently insignificant social gesture can be used to think through the very question of being. And both are forms of sociology.

There is a sense of 'magic' or mysticism in this—or at least an element of the personal, rather than the objective. Certainly sociologists do enter into a relationship with the objects of their research which can become 'personalised'; because they invest in it, and because they are immersed in it, the data can come to take on an almost human aspect, which can make it seem objec-tive rather than framed. Sociologists can overcome this by applying techniques that allow us to break with common sense or intuitive understandings: to undertake a logical critique of ideas, apply statistical tests, develop and apply sets of abstract criteria for describing and measuring a social practice, and not apply features of the most obvious individuals to a group as a whole. In short, we should treat the world under observation as an entirely unknown world (as Durkheim has suggested sociologists do), and constantly test the limits of our methods and position.

Of course, the nature of sociology—which is to ask questions of people, and record social practices and comments—makes it virtually impossible to achieve a neutral, objective position. But still, a researcher who has thought through the meanings of any questions in a questionnaire, and who has theorised the method employed, is more likely to understand the sorts of problems that will inevitably come up in any answers he or she receives. As an example of how easy it is to misunderstand and misapply research techniques, Bourdieu points out that the act of asking a question in a survey implies that everyone and anyone can have an opinion, and that their opinions are of equal value. This is, he writes, 'a naively democratic sentiment' (1979a: 124) because the act of asking a question implicitly requires everyone asked to give some sort of answer, whether their opinions are valid or not, and whether the question is important to them or not. Because it is in a formal survey, the question will seem to be one that is worth asking, and hence worth answering. This practice of surveys and questionnaires may help to construct social discourses (because in the act of asking the questions, they focus social attention on the object of the question) and to reduce complex social relations to a single question or questionnaire that cannot possibly take into account all the differences between and among the people surveyed, or all the nuances of meaning and sense they would be able to offer. So what we get out of questionnaires, he suggests, is not *public* opinion, but 'mobilized opinion, formulated opinion, pressure groups mobilized around a system of interest' (1979a: 129).

Still, to counterbalance all these warnings about the importance of theorising and objectifying one's position as a researcher, Bourdieu does point out that the best way to 'do' sociology is to get past what he calls the 'epistemological preliminaries', and to conduct the craft of sociology as a practice, one that gradually becomes internalised so that the researcher becomes what Bourdieu terms a 'reflexive' practitioner.

The reflexive sociologist

For Bourdieu, as we noted above, one of the most important 'tools' in the sociological toolkit is the ability to objectify one's own position, to defamiliarise one's view of the world, to see and hear not what one expects to see and hear, but what can objectively be identified as being present. And though any sociology textbook will insist on the importance of objectivity in social research, Bourdieu is perhaps the most closely associated with the development of techniques, ways of thinking, and habits of research that can minimise bias and self-blindness.

There are two main issues—or rather, two main *objects*—in this approach to social research and scientific objectivity. The first is, obviously, the need to test one's own position and perspective as a researcher, and the other is the need to question the very foundations of the sociological method. Let us look at the first question.

There is, Bourdieu argues, no neutral question or analytical device available to sociologists. The very act of asking a question as a sociologist implies that there is a problem, and sets the parameters for how that question should be answered. For instance, single parents do not 'exist' as a sociological category, or problem, unless there are social scientists around to reflect on them—and social scientists, moreover, who believe in the idea of the two-parent nuclear family as the norm. So any research question is inevitably shot through with ideological perspectives.

It is also shot through with what Bourdieu calls 'intellectualist bias'. He means by this that the act of observing the social world involves framing that observation first through our own preconceptions, and secondly through changing it, from being thought of as the social space in which we live, into an object of research. When we look with what he calls a 'theoretical gaze', we separate ourselves, conceptually, from the world observed. We engage in a kind of suspension of disbelief which allows us to behave as though we truly have a doubly privileged position—of not being affected by the world we are studying, and of not having to recognise that our view of the world is one predicated on theory rather than lived experience.

There is another side to this notion of intellectual bias. We have, Bourdieu argues, 'an interest in disinterestedness' (1993b: 49); in other words, it is in our interests not to pursue research that is driven by the desire for money or for political power. However, we are often driven by the fact that a problem has become fashionable in our intellectual world, so we have an interest in the problems that seem to us to be interesting. All our colleagues are writing about it, conferences are held to explore it, publications come out about it—and then, just as suddenly, it ceases to be interesting, whether or not it ceases to be a social problem. In the mid-1990s, for instance, the question of citizenship, of what it means to be a citizen, and of how being a citizen affects a person's worldview and life chances, became terribly important. By 2000, you would have been hard pressed to find a conference on the topic, or a special issue of a journal dedicated to it. People have not stopped being citizens, but it no longer seems as interesting to researchers because it's no longer on the agenda, and so it is no longer 'worthwhile' to research it.

The second issue at stake here is that even if the social researcher is able to be fully reflexive and sort out personal interest and personal bias, 'the subject of science is part of the object of science' (1993b: 42). As sociologists, we are 'the subjects of science'—the ones operating social science. But we are also people caught within the discourses, the logics, the rules and the values of the *field* of sociology, and hence we are simultaneously its objects. We might have cleared our research of all personal interest, but because we are still part of a field and a discipline, both the objective gaze that we bring to bear on the 'problem', and the research methodology we apply, are themselves tainted by 'interest'.

So it is important to be clear about what Bourdieu means by reflexivity, particularly within a sociological context (there is a more generalised 'definition' of this concept in Chapter 3). It is not just turning the spotlight on oneself. Important as it is to understand why we see the world the way we see it, and what we may have invested in our research project, sociology is full of what Bourdieu calls 'the key filters that alter sociological perception' (1992d: 38–9)—the values and attitudes are encoded in the very language of sociology itself.

In explaining how to achieve reflexivity, Bourdieu points to four main elements. The first is a standard in any sociology: we must develop an intellectual and theoretical framework that will provide a basis for each piece of research work, including the ethics and values enshrined in the social issue being analysed by the researcher. The second does not look at the researcher, but at what 'truths', or what unconscious or unexamined beliefs, are encoded in the very tools of analysis—everything from 'grand theories' (for example, the views of the 'fathers' of sociology) to methods of gathering data. Third, he points out that social research should always be a collective undertaking (within reason, the more people and hence the more perspectives involved in a project, the more likely it is that they will test one another's world views, and 'balance out' each other's biases). Finally, he provides the assurance that testing the social unconscious inscribed in social research will not damage sociology and sociological ways of knowing, but refine and strengthen them.

Sociological reflexivity offers a way of overcoming the various forms of bias, and is also a way of addressing the ongoing scientific arguments about whether or not social science is a 'real' science. Reflexivity should, he suggests, be applied to science in progress; not as a way of ascertaining whether the research project is 'really' scientific, but as a way of achieving what Gaston Bachelard calls 'an approximated, that is to say, rectified, knowledge' (cited in 1991c: 8). In other words, not even the most rigorous science is going to be able to find 'truth'; but by ascertaining the conditions under which things come to *seem* true, determining the processes of testing for error, and taking a reflexive attitude to the underpinning ideologies of science itself, we can achieve something that is close to an accurate rendering of the research problem.

In effect Bourdieu calls for a sociology of sociology—developing a critique of sociology's knowledges, testing sociology's research methods, and 'bringing to light the unconscious presuppositions and begged questions of a theoretical tradition' (1991c: 69).

Scientific reason and scientific method

Bourdieu is very committed, as we have noted, to breaking away from the tyranny of what is called 'common sense' in the interests of constructing a scientific object, because common sense is just that—senses, notions and representations shared by all, but tested by none. And this is why he uses (as so many students and other writers have complained) very difficult language, highly convoluted sentences, and words taken out of their conventional meanings or contexts and used in new ways. 'Ordinary' language, he argues, has built into it all the standard 'truths' of our society, and using everyday language makes it difficult to read beyond the unconscious acceptance of whatever stands, at a given moment in history, as 'the truth', or the doxa. Sociology—especially Bourdieu's sociology—is difficult to read because of its use of a relatively obscure and even 'jargonistic' language, which forces readers to pay attention to the ideas inscribed in that language, rather than read what amounts to received ideas because everyday language has those ideas built into it. Sociology is also difficult to read, he suggests, because it seems very close to both philosophy and the 'already known' aspects of social life, and yet it is based on empirical research and, often, the use of statistics: without careful training, readers simply will not be able to understand this aspect. A lack of literacy with regard to statistics means people will often confuse what is probable with what is definite, so that they really can't understand the points being made in sociology. So, when people complain that his writing is not clear, he responds that clarity often obscures the very specific statements being made in sociological writing. And besides, clarity typically equals 'the reinforcement of the self-evidences of common sense or the certainties of fanaticism' (1993b: 21). Consequently, he argues, his concern is not for 'literary quality' but for rigorous research and reporting.

This does not mean, though, that he sees scientific language or scientific logic as a magic wand that allows scientists to 'cut through' common sense and the received ideas of everyday language, and find 'the truth'. Indeed, much of his writing is given over to problematising 'scientific reason' as something that is both just as blind, and just as 'interested', as common sense. And this is particularly true for sociology, because sociology deals to so great an extent with everyday things—family arrangements, school systems, community structures. This means that we come to sociological reports about such matters with a sense of familiarity, with far greater pre-judgements than most of us would bring to the results of research in, say, quantum physics.

To complicate things further, sociology and the other human sciences are really the only sciences that deal with speaking subjects rather than speechless objects like J-curves, atoms or cattle dogs. It is frighteningly easy for sociologists to put into or take out of the mouths of their respondents exactly what they want to hear; and it is frighteningly common for sociologists and the subjects they study to see the world not as it is, but as they think it should be; not as it is, but in terms of the values attached to its various aspects. And the ever-presence of self-evidences based on common sense or unexamined prior knowledge means that sociologists have constantly to struggle against the temptation to conduct what Bourdieu calls 'spontaneous sociology'.

The way to break with the tendency to apply spontaneous sociology is to have a very clear understanding of the principles which ground sociological (empirical) method, and consciously to think through the presuppositions of each research method or technique used. This, of course, propels Bourdieu's calls for the methodological rigour and self-reflexive sociology that we discussed above. But objectivity or neutrality is not enough on its own to assure a social scientist of rigorous work. Bourdieu warns of the difficulties in being able to take up and maintain the 'neutral' position which is a founding principle of all science. In fact, Bourdieu writes, the search for an ethically neutral position can produce quite the reverse. As an example of this, he points the finger at those cultural theorists who treat all cultural practices ('folk songs, Bach cantatas, or pop songs' are those he cites in 1991c: 47) as though they can be understood without at the same time understanding the values attached to them by particular social groups.

Because sociologists are dealing so often with commonplace or everyday social practices, it is very difficult to find the right line between 'objectivity' and the naive experience of the thing under investigation. And these two oppositions are reflected in the two distinct logics applied in sociology—the logic of discovery, and the logic of validation. The discovery moment is often relegated to the world of chance or 'the non-rational', while validation is regarded as genuinely 'scientific'. Not surprisingly, Bourdieu discounts the idea that discovery is based on intuition rather than scientific reason; or that validation is purely scientific, and able to keep itself distinct from interest and intuition. He cites Gaston Bachelard's claim that 'the scientific fact is won, constructed, and confirmed' (in 1991c: 11), rather than being the cool, neutral or objective findings from investigation of a research question, to support his assertion that the use of empiricism does not automatically assure that 'science' has been done.

For Bourdieu, discovery is every bit as 'scientific' as validation, because it comes out of a social philosophy which, because it is the basis of speculation which leads to the construction of a hypothesis and then a research program (that is, the scientific act), is necessarily scientific. And empiricism is not necessarily scientific—it only meets these conditions if its theoretical principles are clearly understood and well thought out (that is, if the social philosophy which drives the work is sound). It is important to bear this in mind when undertaking a sociological research project, because standard empiricism tends to force a stability on the variables being measured and tested that may not be justified. It 'forgets' the importance of the differing contexts in which those variables are being measured, and can easily rely on an untested assumption that what a variable means is constant across decades—for instance, assuming that being an artist means the same in 2001 as it did in 1901, or in 1701. The main problem he identifies with 'scientific reason' is that what is really at stake in scientific work is 'the monopoly of *scientific competence*' (1975: 257); not the search for objective truth, but competition for scientific capital—that is, status, prestige, contacts, publications and whatever else has value within the scientific field.

Bourdieu deals with the false dichotomy between empiricism and construction through the sociological method he uses. This, according to his co-researcher and author Loïc Wacquant, includes the use of 'a manner of posing problems, in a parsimonious set of conceptual tools and procedures for constructing objects and for transfering knowledge gleaned in one area of inquiry into another' (Wacquant, in Bourdieu 1992d: 5). It is, in fact, a *relational* approach to social research—which again shows how much his methodology has developed since his early structuralism-influenced research in Algeria.

Rather than privileging invention over validation, collectivities over individuals, or systems over subjects, Bourdieu takes pains to show how each is related to, and dependent upon, the other. He argues, for instance, that research is (and must be) both empirical (because it is an act of observing social phenomena) and theoretical (because it depends on conceptualising the systems of relations that underpin those social phenomena). For instance, while it may be very straightforward to construct samples for research into the population of artists, how do we define 'artists'? How do we decide who to include, and who to exclude, without some conceptual or theoretical framework for making these sorts of distinctions?

The point in this research approach is to insist that research is a 'rational endeavour'—incorporating both theory and empiricism—and not a 'mystical quest' (1992d: 218). Its rationality is bound up with a very practical approach to detail. Bourdieu lists such details as locating reliable informants, deciding the best way of approaching them and explaining the aims of the research, and above all, learning how to 'enter' the world as an observer and, to some extent at least, a participant. So he urges researchers not to fetishise theory, not to consider those concepts which we have argued are so closely associated with his work, such as field, habitus and capital, as significant in themselves, but to see them as concepts that can and should be put to work in making sense of the world that comes under the sociologist's gaze.

He points out how he actually uses such concepts. 'Field', he says, 'functions as a *pense-bête*, a memory-jogger: it tells me that

I must, at every stage, make sure that the object I have given myself is not enmeshed in a network of relations that assign its most distinctive properties' (1992d: 228). What this allows us to do, he goes on to say, is to overcome the temptation to view the social world as substance, and remember that it is, above all, relational. And when using field as a research concept, he undertakes three distinct but connected acts. He analyses the relation of the field under question to the field of power; he maps out the positions available within the field, and especially those positions that are the subject of competition for field-specific capital; and, finally, he analyses the habitus of the individuals who occupy the field to determine how their dispositions have come into being and have been internalised, and what sorts of tendencies they generate.

This is not, of course, simple or self-evident. If we view the world relationally, we necessarily make sense of social realities only in terms of the relative ownership of various forms of capital by institutions and individuals in the fields we investigate. This can be very limiting, but the limits can be overcome if we interview everyone relevant to the social question or problem being researched. And this brings its own dangers of becoming reductive, or spontaneous, or (to use Bourdieu's other term), regressing to the 'reality' of preconstructed social units (1992d: 230).

He suggests researchers can guard against these tendencies by using a very simple instrument—producing a table that lists all the pertinent aspects of the individuals and institutions in the field being researched. So, he will list all the relevant institutions, for instance, on a row, and then, in the early stages of studying them, draw up columns for each significant property that attaches to any of the institutions. Then he will check each institution for the presence or absence of each property. By collapsing columns that contain functionally equivalent properties, he is left with lists of properties that are analytically relevant; and from this point can investigate the field with some confidence that he has overcome his own preconceptions, or any reductive tendencies.

The point of research, for Bourdieu, is to make sense of why things happen, what are their social reasons for being, and what are the bases for the presence of social distinctions. He writes

(1992a) that distinctions which seem to be based on objective differences (such as gender or race, for instance) are the most difficult to disavow because they seem natural and obvious. Of course, there are never in fact absolute differences, even in apparently 'natural' distinctions such as gender, because the attributes are always distributed along a continuum—from very 'masculine men' at one end, say, through to very 'feminine women' at the other end, and everyone else somewhere in between. 'Social magic, however, always manages to produce discontinuities out of the continuity' (1992a: 83). And even within the scientific community, similar distinctions are found: 'Our own intellectual apparatus,' he writes, 'believing itself free from all constraint, is full of oppositions of this type . . . When you say "quantitative sociology/qualitative sociology", you are not far from "masculine/feminine"' (1992b: 39). But by ascertaining the 'laws' of the social and the scientific world, and distinguishing between those things that are destiny or nature and those that are social and arbitrary, sociologists can provide better knowledge about the laws and their underpinnings, and can provide the grounds for social change and for greater freedom. This is because if we can identify the ways in which we are actually determined (for instance, by not being able to beat gravity) and the ways in which we are socially determined (by being coded as 'woman' and therefore 'emotional') we are in a better position to take up processes of resistance, and to achieve freedom.

Not that this is straightforward. As Bourdieu says, in the final words in *Craft*:

> To be able to see and describe the world as it is, you have to
> be ready to be always dealing with things that are compli-
> cated, confused, impure, uncertain, all of which runs counter
> to the usual idea of intellectual rigour. (1991c: 259)

What all this means is that just as it is not possible to have a pure distinction between men and women, or between 'natural' and 'social' distinctions, so too it is not possible to separate out theoretical or inventive sociology from empirical or validation sociology in terms of their relative rigour or scientific value. What is necessary, rather, is that sociologists practise 'epistemological vigilance'—reflecting on their own social contexts, social conditions, ways of thinking and prejudices that colour how they view the world, and applying a carefully wrought empiricism along with a rigorous theoretical framework to their research.

Conclusion

- Bourdieu's sociology comes out of a tradition that includes not just the 'fathers' of sociology, but also social philosophy and the philosophy of science; in fact, he takes what he needs from any source he considers appropriate for the task at hand.
- He is, nevertheless, committed to rational and empirical research methodologies, but always wary of the dangers of over-reliance on research techniques.
- Because of the inevitable flaws in research—and especially the risk of bias—he stresses the need for a reflexive sociology.

Further reading

Bourdieu, Pierre 1975, 'The specificity of the scientific field and the social conditions of the progress of reason' *Social Science Information*, 14/6, pp. 19–47

Certeau, Michel de 1984, *The Practice of Everyday Life*, trans. Steven Rendall, University of California Press, Berkeley, Ch 4

Jenkins, Richard 1992, *Pierre Bourdieu*, Routledge, London & New York, Ch 4

Robbins, Derek 1991, *The Work of Pierre Bourdieu: Recognizing Society*, Open University Press, Milton Keynes, Ch 2

5

Government and bureaucracy

The eighteenth-century English philosopher David Hume wrote, with reference to government, that:

> Nothing is as astonishing for those who consider human affairs with a philosophic eye than to see the ease with which the many will be governed by the few and to observe the implicit submission with which men revoke their own sentiments and passions in favor of their leaders. (quoted in Bourdieu 1994a: 15)

Bourdieu is perhaps less astonished than Hume, though he is equally interested in the processes and mechanisms by which 'the many' are governed by 'the few'. But while his work is in many ways very politicised, most of his publications don't deal directly with government, or take its various institutions as the focus of attention. All the same, his attitude to the government—which he calls 'the state'—and its bureaucratic mechanisms emerges in works like *Language and Symbolic Power* (1991a), *Practical Reason* (1998d) and *Acts of Resistance* (1998b). In these books he describes government as both a cultural field and a field of power.

We have looked, in Chapter 2, at what is meant by 'cultural field', but need to pause for a moment and consider what 'field of power' means in Bourdieu's terms. The word 'power' is often treated as though it is identical with, or at least emerges from, 'government'. But in fact there is a difference between the two

85

terms and the two fields. For Bourdieu, as we have already noted, 'field' is a metaphor for the (metaphorical) space in which we can identify institutions, agents, discourses, practices, values, and so on. Consequently, we can talk about the 'field' of government, and point to ministries and departments, parliaments and senates, offices and officers as well as legislation, policy and other discourses and practices.

So there are all kinds of concrete instances associated with our use of the term. But when we use the term 'field of power' in Bourdieu's sense, we think of it not as the site of institutions and institutional practices, but as a metaphor for the ways in which fields actually conduct themselves—particularly dominant fields, such as the government, or the economic field. The government has a responsibility (as we will discuss in this chapter) to regulate, manage and police the national community; and power is the mechanism it applies to fulfil this responsibility. In other words, the government is not the field of power, but is one of the sites in which power operates. This means we can understand 'power' as a meta-field, or a macro-concept, to describe the ways in which individuals and institutions within dominant fields relate to one another and to the whole social field.

We see these sorts of relationships, for instance, when the state bank or exchequer adjusts the value of the local currency relative to its trading partners, or when it moves interest rates up or down. The bank shows in these sorts of acts the *traces* of power moving across both government and finance. So, to put it another way, we can think of the field of power as a configuration of capital— not necessarily economic capital, but any sorts of resources, including things like social and professional contacts, personal or institutional status and anything else that has value and translates into the ability to make things happen. And all the usual suspects inhabit this 'field'—government and bureaucracy, economic and financial institutions, schools and universities, the professions, the armed services, the media; in other words, all the fields that overdetermine other fields. Think again, for instance, of the state bank. We could justifiably locate it within the economic field, as it is the primary institution charged to regulate the economy (including interest rates, currency exchange rates, the amount of cash in circulation, and so on). And it is able to 'make things happen'—to decide on and implement monetary policy—because it has the sort of 'capital' (economic, social and symbolic) that allows it to do so. But it doesn't act alone. It must respond to the other dominant fields: to the government, which authorises it; to the financial sector, which it manages and which influences its decisions; and even, perhaps, to the media, which reports on those decisions. So it isn't necessarily powerful in itself, or in terms of its own specific field. Its power comes from its relationship to other dominant fields, and from its position as part of the meta-field—the field of power—which acts on other fields and influences their practices.

Government becomes the marker of the field of power, the site from which it (apparently) emerges, because of its social position as that set of institutions, discourses, acts and codes, and practices which regulate and conduct the activities of virtually all other fields and institutions. But government isn't actually the starting point for power. Any military or civilian coup is a demonstration of how slippery power can be, in practice. In May 2000, for instance, the government of the small Pacific nation of Fiji was taken hostage by a disaffected (and armed) individual who decided he had a better way of managing and regulating Fiji than its elected parliament—an instance of power emerging from somewhere other than the field of government, and able to leave its mark on that field. But the government is, nonetheless, perhaps most dominant of the dominant, the field whose institutions, discourses, practices, technologies and general organisation provide it with the means to impose particular beliefs and understandings on the whole social field. And Bourdieu's interest in its structure and functions is neither neutral nor objective. As our earlier discussion of his attitude to social research should indicate, his interest in government is driven by the critical imperative to test it out and, where possible, make changes.

We see this in the very critical tone of his publications and lectures on governments in the late 1990s. In *Acts of Resistance*, for instance, or in the article 'On the cunning of imperialist reason' (1999b), he outlines the many ways in which, as he sees it, the modern state is abrogating its responsibilities, especially to disadvantaged groups in society. In these works we can detect an attitude to the state that is marked by a sense of frustration (because the government isn't doing what it claims to do). We can also identify an attitude of what he calls 'hyperbolic doubt'. In fact, he writes, 'when it comes to the state, one never doubts enough' (1998d: 36).

In this chapter we outline Bourdieu's approach to the state and its institutions. We 'map' his writings on the narratives and social practices that make communities appear natural and ahistorical, and governments seem to be the owners of legitimate authority. We pay particular attention to Bourdieu's work on how language is used as an instrument of symbolic power. And finally we explore his writings on bureaucracy, which is the instrument by which the government operationalises its programs.

Imaginary states

One of the enduring beliefs in most societies is that 'the community'—be it local or national—has a 'real' existence, an identity as tangible as the continents, for instance, and as natural as the Amazon forest or the Rhine river. Along with this notion of the real identity of the geographical space is the idea that the people who make up the community are an identifiable group, one that is homogeneous, coherent and possessed of common marks of identity (shared traditions, similar skin colour, identical language and so on). But as writers including Bourdieu have argued, and as civil wars during the 1990s in places like the African country of Rwanda or the former Yugoslav province of Bosnia showed, a community isn't natural or inevitable. Rather, it is constructed by a series of discourses about 'society'; its boundaries are established arbitrarily as the result of (often) centuries of conflict; and the community (both land and people) emerge as 'real' only as the result of a series of societal practices.

The existence of this 'community' depends on both its members and outsiders sharing a belief that it exists. Britain, for instance, is certainly a social reality because we can locate it on the world map, we meet people who tell us they are 'English' or

'British', and in university courses we can study 'English literature' or 'British history'. The American writer Bill Bryson gives
us an example of the way that 'Britain' and 'the British' come to
have a real identity, in his 1997 book *Notes From a Small Island*:

> Suddenly, in the space of a moment, I realized what it was
> that I loved about Britain—which is to say, all of it. Every last
> bit of it, good and bad—old churches, country lanes, people
> saying 'Mustn't grumble' and 'I'm terribly sorry but,' people
> apologizing to me when I conk them with a careless elbow,
> milk in bottles, beans on toast, haymaking in June, seaside
> piers, Ordinance Survey maps, tea and crumpets, summer
> showers and foggy winter evenings—every bit of it.

In this description, Bryson presents features and qualities that we
are meant to identify as immediately, recognisably British, and
obviously and inevitably different from those that pertain to
people called, say, Croatian or Italian. And those of us who grew
up reading A.E. Ransome stories, or watching BBC television
shows, can 'recognise' these features as peculiarly British. But this
only works if we forget the many differences among the people
who make up 'the British'—those who speak little or no English,
for instance, those who do in fact grumble, or those who won't
under any circumstances apologise. It also depends on our forgetting the history of Britain, which would remind us that 'the British'
includes many peoples, with many languages, many geographical locations, and many different ways of naming themselves: as
Welsh, for instance, or Scottish rather than British. All have at one
point or another been the subject of considerable struggle or open
battle. Films like *Braveheart, My Beautiful Laundrette, Lock, Stock and
Two Smoking Barrels* or *Naked* give us a very different vision of
Britain and the British, a vision of a fragmented community
holding together people with dramatically varying social, racial,
linguistic, ethnic and class identities, a Britain that is very far from
the familiar and comforting Britain Bill Bryson sees.

The idea that a group called 'us' really exists, and is made up
of people who have identifiable and shared characteristics, is
found in most nations, and repeated in the calls to arms of any

number of politicians and social commentators around the world. But what Bourdieu and other writers on national community point out is that 'the nation' (say, 'the British') exists only in the stories and collective beliefs of groups of people. Once they cease to believe in it—as happened during the 1990s in the former Yugoslavia—its identity melts into air. This means that we cannot understand local and national communities as either natural or coherent; rather, they are stitched together as effects of the stories, discourses, practices and authorised values of the various fields which constitute them. Nor are they homogeneous. Any national community is based on division (one social class or other group is carefully separated from, and identified as different from, another) and differentiation (any one nation-state is distinguished from territories and social groups beyond its boundaries). So every national community is a political, rather than a natural or historically inevitable, entity.

Because national entities are political entities, nation-states are necessarily founded on violence—or rather, on several forms of violence. Many nations, for instance, came into being as the result of physical violence: invasion, war or colonisation. Another form of violence is the discursive one, in which only official histories of the nation are told and alternative histories are 'forgotten' or obscured. In the United States, for instance, one important founding story is that the Pilgrims travelled to the 'new' world to escape religious oppression, and to found a community based on principles of faith and freedom. As the records show, it was not long at all before these seekers of freedom were oppressing the local inhabitants, persecuting eccentrics in their own group and enthusiastically practising slavery. But all the same, the Pilgrim/Puritan myth continues to prevail. The many alternative American histories (of native Americans, African- Americans, women, the poor and so on) that appear in publications, comedy routines or films, have the status of what Bourdieu calls 'heterodoxy' (something that challenges the status quo) rather than being seen as 'orthodox', or legitimate.

Bourdieu's ideas help us to make sense of this sort of competition, showing that—to paraphrase Marx's famous statement—the dominant vision of the social world is the vision of dominant groups in the society. So the community's originary acts of violence, as well as the potential 'histories' that were not allowed to emerge (say, that women, African-Americans and native Americans might have been included in the 'all men' of the United States Declaration of Independence, or that the Americas were not 'new', and did not need to be 'discovered'), are 'forgotten'. 'Official' histories which support dominant practices are the ones that circulate and are repeated in authoritative publications and practices, and only these 'official' histories are (officially) remembered. And in this process of constructing an official history, the present shape of the society comes to seem both natural and inevitable.

The government as a cultural field

Let us move now from considering the national community to look at what Bourdieu calls the state—the government—and its relation to the community and to powerful groups and individuals in that community. It is important to keep in mind that although he constantly points out how effective the ideas of dominant groups are in establishing legitimate views of the world, he does not suggest that the state is simply a tool of powerful social groups. Instead, he writes, the state can be understood as a cultural field in its own right, one that is certainly powerful, but is not necessarily identical with the ruling class, or with other powerful fields. For Bourdieu, the government has its own institutions, discourses, agents, positions, values and so on that are relatively independent of other powerful social groups and institutions. This provides it with an objective existence (seen in its institutions and legal mechanisms), and a subjective existence (seen in the ways in which the 'state' structures how people perceive themselves and their world). And this combination of objective and subjective existence means we tend to believe that the state, like the national community it governs, has always been there.

Bourdieu writes that as a state develops its structures and authority, it also develops:

a concentration of physical force and a concentration of economic force—the two go together, you need money to make war, to police the country and so on, and you need a police force to collect money. Next comes a concentration of cultural capital, and then a concentration of authority. (1998b: 32)

In the process of coming into being and establishing its structures and identity, the state increasingly exerts power over the people who have now become classified as its citizens. This happens, he writes, because the systems of organisation that develop in a nation's laws and policies, the bureaucratic procedures that operationalise these and the educational institutions that train us how to think, are all tools by which 'the state molds mental structures and imposes common principles of vision and division' (1994a: 7).

This sets up a rather grim view of modern society, because it seems to suggest that the government, even in a liberal-democratic nation, is inevitably oppressive. People living in liberal democracies might well dispute this, and point out that though the state may have a monopoly on violence—having the exclusive right to police and punish its citizens and to protect its borders through armed force—it does not usually exercise this overtly or coercively; at least, not against those who have sufficient social and symbolic capital to offer resistance.

This does not, however, mean that governments are, first and foremost, mechanisms of control. The French theorist on power and governmentality, Michel Foucault, wrote that the state can't behave in a dictatorial or totalitarian way, because this would contradict its discourses of a commitment to participatory democracy. Instead, he argues, the state concerns itself with managing, organising and otherwise regulating 'individuals, goods and wealth'. In other words, the state may indeed not be going around arresting and imprisoning its citizens or subjects for overtly political reasons, but because it 'owns' the rights of legislative and administrative organisation, it *in fact* controls virtually everything we do. It is the state, for instance, that organises what food is produced and how; where, how and by whom that food may be sold; and how much of our income we have available to spend on food. It regulates who we marry (at least, what gender of person we may marry), and when. It regulates how and where we give birth; how we raise and educate our children; what sort of cars we drive; and where and how we can drive them. And because it can do all this without pointing a gun at our heads, Foucault argues, the state exercises its violence on us with our consent, and indeed with our complicity.

How does the state achieve this complicity? This takes us back to Bourdieu's notion of habitus. Habitus, as we pointed out in Chapter 2, does not apply only to the individual subject. Whole communities can be identified as having a collective habitus, characterised by shared perspectives on the world, relatively common sets of values and shared dispositions to believe and behave in particular ways. The state partially orchestrates this collective habitus by creating the conditions under which certain things come to be viewed as natural and inevitable (capitalist systems of economic organisation, for instance) and others unthinkable (uncontrolled immigration, for instance). It does this also because power and capital are both concentrated in the state, and so it can establish what constitutes acceptable behaviour and how deviance should be punished—a powerful mechanism for ensuring that its truths come to be internalised and accepted as general truths. But perhaps the most effective way that the state creates and orchestrates this collective habitus is by ensuring that it is seen by the people it governs as being 'the voice of the people', which gives it legitimate authority to rule us, and even to exercise violence against us.

In the film *Monty Python and the Holy Grail* we see this approach to government worked out in the scene where King Arthur approaches some peasants and addresses them as their natural superior—their king. The peasants, though, are members of an anarcho-syndicalist commune, and dispute his rulership and his principle of government. When Arthur tries to impose his authority, they reject him and his claims: 'I didn't vote for you,' says one. Nor can he assert divine right to rule: 'Strange women lying in ponds distributing swords is no basis for a system of government. Supreme executive power derives from a mandate from the masses, not from some farcical aquatic ceremony,' says another. Inevitably, the two parties can't reach any accord because they have no shared habitus, and King Arthur resorts to verbal and physical abuse before leaving hastily—a wonderful example of the limits on government, and the importance of the citizens' complicity in their own subjection.

While King Arthur is, of course, the first really important monarch in English myth, his kingdom of Camelot was in many ways like a modern democracy because it promised general rights and universal justice, and so gave the appearance of being 'for everyone', while in fact being the domain of the dominant. Bourdieu offers several reasons why, in an apparently participatory context, some groups and people are dominated and others are dominant. First, people can only participate in the political field if they have the resources—the time and money—to do so; and the dominated are less likely than the dominant to possess this sort of capital. Think, for example, of any United States presidential campaign over the past one hundred years—the candidates have been wealthy men and, with very few exceptions, have been white and Protestant. So, in the nation that has carried the flame of democracy over the twentieth century, where 'any boy can grow up to be president', only a very narrow sector of society—the dominant—has provided presidential candidates, because only they have the time and money to compete in that race.

Second, anyone wishing to participate in the political field also needs social capital—the 'right' social contacts—and cultural capital—a 'feel for the game' of politics. The mockumentary *Bob Roberts* depicts a corrupt candidate for a senatorial position who consistently judged the mood of the people to whom he was appealing, ensured he was seen in the right places (schools, churches), and even arranged for his own fake assassination attempt in order to win the hearts of the voters. Not only did Bob Roberts have a 'feel for the game', but he had contacts in media, public relations, politics, security and so on who were able to smooth his path to the Senate, and ultimately (at least implicitly) to the White House.

The need for social and cultural capital of course also excludes dominated individuals and groups from active political participation because typically they will not have had much involvement with politics, or have the contacts or the confidence that comes with possession of that sort of capital, and so are more likely than dominant individuals to 'leave it to the professionals'.

Language and power

We have referred to the fact that the state uses discourses and stories to establish and maintain its dominance over other powerful social fields; in other words, the whole national community—individuals, organisations and major institutions—are engaged in competition to become the most dominant, a competition the government usually wins. At bottom, this competition is more for *symbolic* than for physical and economic control, because what is at stake in the struggle is the right to impose on others a particular view of the world. And because the struggle is symbolic, it is language which is both the battleground and the weapon. This is what Bourdieu refers to when he writes about language and symbolic power. Language is not powerful in and of itself, but it becomes powerful when it is used in particular ways, or by particular groups and institutions.

Language can be used as a battlefield and as a weapon because it is, Bourdieu writes, both a 'structuring structure' (it provides the means for understanding the world) and a 'structured structure' (it is the medium by which these understandings are communicated). And this is why the modern democratic state is able to retain all the power of the old autocratic state: because it controls 'legitimate language'—the structures and the media of meaning-making and understanding—it is able to ensure that its citizens will accept its right to rule them. With control of what counts as the legitimate language comes symbolic power, that power which does not take the form of physical deeds, but which brings things into being by naming them, and by making people see and believe a particular vision of the world. It is, Bourdieu writes, 'that invisible power which can be exercised only with the complicity of those who do not want to know that they are subject to it' (1991a: 164).

The important point in this, for Bourdieu, is that symbolic power is not recognised *as* power. Rather, it seems to be similar

95

to physical laws like gravity: we do not treat gravity as oppressive, but as inevitable; and we obey it without thinking about it because it seems the only thing to do. In the same way, we comply with the dominant vision of the world not because we necessarily agree with it, or because it is in our interests, but because there does not seem to be any alternative. And often, Bourdieu points out, we may not even be conscious of complying with the dominant discourses. His research into dominated social groups, reported in *The Weight of the World* (1999a), or into the relations beween men and women as reported in *Masculine Domination* (2001), shows that particular people—those from dominated groups, women—often just accept that the way things are is the way things should be, or have always been. He uses the term 'doxa' to explain this apparently surprising practice of accepting things without realising that one is being oppressed, or that there are any alternatives to the status quo. 'I have always been surprised', he writes in the opening line of *Masculine Domination:*

> by what might be called the *paradox of doxa*—the fact that the order of the world as we find it, with its one-way streets and its no entry signs, whether literal or figurative, its obligations and its penalties, is broadly respected; that there are not more transgressions and subversions . . .; or, still more surprisingly, that the established order, with its relations of domination . . . ultimately perpetuates itself so easily. (2001: 1)

Doxa is the term he applies to the 'objectively real truth' (which is defended in orthodoxy, and attacked in heterodoxy) and which he uses to explain the ways in which subjects adjust themselves to ideology's rules, even when it causes them suffering. The doxic attitude', Bourdieu writes:

> does not mean happiness; it means bodily submission, unconscious submission, which may indicate a lot of internalized tension . . . I have discovered a lot of suffering which had been hidden by this smooth working of habitus. It helps people to adjust, but it causes internalized contradictions. (1994b: 276–7)

As he points out in *Language and Symbolic Power,* and in more recent publications like *The Weight of the World,* 'On the cunning of imperialist reason' (1999b), or *Masculine Domination,* language is the tool used by the state to change the general understanding of the state's responsibility for its citizens. Even in states which have an overt commitment to some socialist values, what he calls 'political codewords and mottoes'—words like 'economic rationalism' or 'neo-liberalism'—are used to describe the downsizing of the state, the reduction of workers' rights and security, and the slashing of social benefits like welfare payments. The frightening thing, he points out, is that it is very difficult to pin down the sources of these changes, because they come to us not in policy documents or organisational philosophy, but in everyday language—in the newspapers and on television, in news reports, documentaries, and current affairs programs. Words like 'independence' are coming to mean that the state need not provide for its people's needs; 'flexibility' means corporations can ignore workers' rights in the interests of higher profits; 'family values' means that the frail, the elderly or the mentally ill can be tipped out of public institutions to be looked after by their families—whether they have families or not, and whether or not their families have any ability to care for them.

Language, especially as it is diffused in everyday discourse, is being used to change subtly the way people understand their relationship to themselves, to each other and to the state. One of the significant mechanisms used by the state to produce this 'doxa' is the bureaucratic institution, and we will turn now to Bourdieu's writings on the bureaucracy.

What is bureaucracy?

At the beginning of this chapter we pointed out that a group exists only when there are sufficient *stories* of its existence (the subjective view) and *institutions* committed to its existence (the objective view). The bureaucracy is very important in this regard, because it is the largest and perhaps the most powerful institution of government. In fact, Bourdieu writes, it is bureaucrats, 'a state nobility', who 'caused the state to come into being by stating what it should be' (1994a: 15). Not only that; the bureaucracy ensures that the community too has a concrete identity, because it acts as an intermediary between the state and the community, implementing the state's policies, and providing the public with a voice in government.

Bureaucracies are particularly important in liberal democracies because they are the 'proof' that the state is objective, disinterested and legitimate. This is because the bureaucracy provides for that separation of powers which is the basis for liberal democracy, and because bureaucracy is characterised by accountability, meticulous record-keeping and attention to procedure. This means that the everyday management of society, which is in the hands of the bureaucrats rather than the politicians, seems to be objective and neutral, not 'contaminated' by the motivated, particular interest of politicians, political parties or lobby groups.

The German sociologist Max Weber suggests that bureaucracy has a more negative function—that it serves government, industry and other dominant groups, rather than the public interest. But many contemporary writers (including Bourdieu) argue that the bureaucracy is neither a tool of the dominant, nor just an intermediary between state and society; nor is it the guardian of the people's rights. In fact, the bureaucracy is a powerful field in its own right: it does not just instrumentalise government policy, but also interprets and sometimes inspires it. And although bureaucracy takes the official position that it is committed to a universal, rather than a personal or political interest, and although, under the neo-liberal or corporatist government model, bureaucrats are not really independent from the elected government, many public servants will argue (though usually only in private) that they are more concerned with their own careers and the status of their own ministries than with the public good. Or, at least, they will identify the public good as that which is also in the interests of their own careers and their own ministry, rather than strictly following the governing party's line.

We can understand how bureaucrats move from a stated commitment to objectivity and the general interest to an actual commitment to a personal interest if we understand the bureaucracy as a field, with its own laws, values and sets of practices, internal structures, systems and discourses. It also, Bourdieu points out, generates in its members a bureaucratic habitus that means they accept its legitimacy as self-evident. It can 'capture' its members thus because:

> The fundamental law of bureaucratic apparatuses is that the apparatus gives everything (including power over the apparatus) to those who give it everything and expect everything from it because they themselves have nothing or are nothing outside it. (1991a: 216)

In other words, the bureaucracy demands of its members complete adherence to its laws and forms. So someone who joins the public service for a job or a career, or through a commitment to the regulation and government of society, will almost inevitably come under the spell of the system, and begin to 'be thought by' the system rather than to think it—to act on behalf of 'the system', rather than on behalf of one's own values or one's group's interests.

Bureaucracy and the dominated

This brings us to another effect of bureaucracy, which is its role in ensuring that 'the many' are prepared to be governed by 'the few'. This is, Bourdieu points out, because under representative (bureaucratic) democracy, everyone apparently has a voice, but they can only be heard if they either engage in social disobedience or hand over to an authorised representative the responsibility for articulating their aspirations and complaints. And typically, it is one of the bureaucratic institutions which becomes this 'authorised representative': the Education Department represents teachers, students and parents, the Ministry of Women's Affairs takes up the interests of women, the Transport Office is the official voice for motorists and other road users, and so on.

The bureaucratic institution is a legitimate spokesperson for these groups, first because it is part of the legitimate government, and second because it is recognised by the community groups which it represents. Its presence, and activity, means the group's interests are able to take on a social form, and become something worth hearing, something that has a 'universal' rather than a merely personal concern. As Bourdieu writes, having a bureaucrat speak on your behalf means 'the simple cry of revolt or indignation becomes a voice that can get itself recognised as such—as having its share of universality and therefore of humanity' (1986a: 302).

But it can also mean you become dispossessed and silenced even further. We pointed out earlier that the more dominated a group or individual may be, the less likely it is that they will feel able, or in fact be able, to participate robustly in the public domain. And, Bourdieu suggests, dominated or 'dispossessed' people tend to rely on delegates to represent them, and so give their voice over to an official spokesperson. A dispossessed group may be brought into visibility through the department or committee which represents their interests, but at the same time its members are further silenced because they are heard only through their spokesperson.

Of course, bureaucracies are not the home only for official government employees. Many bureaucratic organisations also have committees and boards on which members of the public can sit, and from which they can contribute to decisions about policies that affect their community of interest. While this is typically presented as a prime example of participatory democracy—because 'the people' are having an actual voice in government—Bourdieu takes a rather cynical view of this practice. He points out that public committees are not really participatory, because what tends to happen is that the representatives become imbued with the 'truth' of the state, and forget the interests of themselves and of their community; their habitus changes to become more like that of a member of the bureaucracy than a member of their own community. So representatives co-opted onto state committees risk becoming peers not of their own community of interest, but of the bureaucratic structure. This has often been a complaint raised against women or people of colour who sit on committees—not just that they are the 'token' woman or 'token' black, but that they start thinking like bureaucrats, and forget the interests of the group they are there to represent. This is rather inevitable, because committee members are likely to have an influence in the committee only in so far as they perform like everyone else on the committee, take on the perspectives, discourses and ideologies of the government organisations to which they report, and become more like members of the bureaucracy than like members of their own community of interest.

Even when such representatives resist being caught up in the bureaucratic machine, it is not easy for them to bring about changes; first because bureaucracies are highly structured, and hence highly resistant to change, but also because anyone included on a committee on the grounds of their identity as a member of a marginalised group is, in fact, there only as a 'token'. For instance, a woman nominated to a committee to represent 'women's interests' will not be seen as a 'real' member of the committee, but as being there only to represent women's issues and interests, authorised to speak only on such issues, and thus excluded from full membership. She may indeed speak on all sorts of other issues, but will only be understood as having something to say when the topic is something to do with women—or with gender issues more generally. So, while being co-opted to a bureaucratic committee has all the appearance of equity, it can easily become another point of exclusion if the individual representative is only there as proof that marginalised people have a voice in government.

Government and power

This all presents a rather bleak view of the relationship of the state and its bureaucratic mechanisms to the people. And it is made more bleak still by Bourdieu's insistence, at least in his 1987 and 1994 articles, that the state's point of view has been so thoroughly impressed in the minds of the people, and its authority made to seem so natural and inevitable, that 'resistance is futile'—and unthinkable. For instance, he wrote in 1994 that 'the question of the legitimacy of the state, and of the order it institutes, does not arise except in crisis situations' (1994a: 15)—unless there is a dramatic event, or major crisis, people tend to accept the authority of the government without thinking about it.

Of course, as his research and publication during the second part of the 1990s demonstrates, there have been a number of 'crisis situations' that make it possible for the 'question of the legitimacy of the state' to be raised. Many of these crises he identifies as the direct effect of the state—particularly in France—having abrogated its responsibility to the common good, because 'the state has withdrawn, or is withdrawing, from a number of sectors of social life for which it was previously responsible' (1998b: 2). And this is not a crisis confined to France. The massive strikes in Britain during the Thatcher administration, and the ongoing poverty and unemployment there; the race riots and the abandonment of inner cities to poverty and ghetto-isation in the United States; and the rolling back of social welfare systems in New Zealand and Australia are other trenchant examples of the withdrawal of the state from the disadvantaged, and the social despair and unrest which follows this.

This may suggest a radical change in the role and the identity of the state over the coming decades. As we have argued in this chapter, the state has traditionally been the field of power because it has been able to convince its population that it was there 'for all', and because it has been able to engender a collective habitus, a shared identity and set of dispositions. But if the state blatantly neglects public need, it will no longer be able to present itself as the most effective mechanism for taking care of the universal interest. As Bourdieu writes: 'the social world is riddled with *calls to order* that function as such only for those who are predisposed to heeding them as they *awaken* deeply buried corporeal dispositions, outside the channels of consciousness and calculation' (1994a: 14).

If those corporeal dispositions (produced through the habitus) don't exist, or don't predispose people to respond to the calls to order, then several effects are likely. The first is what we saw from time to time over the 1990s—social unrest, civil

disobedience, or outright riots. Another effect could be classified as a cynical self-interest, as Bourdieu writes: 'One has the
sense now that citizens, feeling themselves ejected from the
state, . . . reject the state, treating it as an alien power to be used
so far as they can to serve their own interests' (1998b: 4–5). And
the final effect is the one he describes in *The Weight of the
World*—that the dominated will simply comply with the established order, and submit themselves to the status quo, despite
their own suffering.

Conclusion

Bourdieu's work on government and bureaucracy explains how
power comes to be understood as legitimate; how a collection of
individuals comes to be formed into a group and to take on existence as a community; and how the state is able to present itself
as natural, inevitable and legitimate. But he also shows that there
is a limit to the extent to which people will obey without questioning the dictates of the state, or the predispositions of their own
habitus to take the collective interest as their own. What this points
to is the importance, for sociologists and other scholars, of continually analysing the 'stories' told by governments and their agents,
and examining how their truth claims are formed and imposed.
With such information, we will be in a better position to make
representations to the government, and actively seek social change.

In this chapter we have discussed:

- The way in which groups and their identities come into being
  as the direct result of stories of identity—and that they do not
  have a 'real' identity outside these stories.
- The mechanisms by which governments are able to institute
  themselves as legitimate authorities—principally by the use
  of symbolic power, or the control of what counts as legitimate
  language, and legitimate representations of reality.
- The role of bureaucracies in implementing government policy
  and in providing a voice for the public—and the extent to
  which they fail to provide for the universal interest.

- The changing nature of the state, in terms of the grounds of its power, and the extent of its responsibility to take care of the universal interest, or the common good.

Further reading

Bourdieu, Pierre 1987, 'What makes a social class? On the theoretical and practical existence of groups', trans. Loïc Wacquant and David Young, *Berkeley Journal of Sociology,* pp. 1–17

Bourdieu, Pierre 1994a, 'Rethinking the state: genesis and structure of the bureaucratic field' *Sociological Theory*, 12, 1, pp. 1–18

Bourdieu, Pierre and Terry Eagleton 1994b, 'Doxa and Common Life: an interview', in Slavoj Zizek ed., *Mapping Ideology*, Verso, London, pp. 265–77

Foucault, Michel 1991, 'Governmentality', in Graham Burchell, Colin Gordon and Peter Miller eds, *The Foucault Effect: Studies in Governmentality*, University of Chicago Press, Chicago pp. 87–104

6

Bourdieu and secondary schools

We pointed out, in Chapter 1, that Bourdieu has made a number of forays into the field of education. This chapter focuses on schooling (particularly secondary schooling), and the following chapter considers the implications of Bourdieu's thought for higher education, particularly universities.

Education is of crucial importance for Bourdieu because it is the mechanism through which the values and relations that make up the social space are passed on from one generation to the next. Accordingly, Bourdieu has devoted much of his research to mapping relations and objective structures within the French school system. Texts such as *Reproduction in Education, Society and Culture* (1977b), which he co-wrote with Jean-Claude Passeron, have been particularly influential.

While the French school system which Bourdieu studies is relatively closed, elitist and intensely competitive in its structure, his ideas still have resonance within apparently open and democratic school systems that are committed to advancing the cause of every child. Consequently, we argue that his ideas are relevant for understanding the school systems of all modern western societies, though it is necessary to consider the particular context that applies within schools in different nations. Bourdieu's own writings encourage this approach; he calls, for example, for 'relational' and 'generative' readings of his work, approaches that allow the models he employs to be applied to what he calls the 'particular case of the possible', or the social relations that pertain in each national or regional context (1998d: 13).

We should note that, as is characteristic of his approach, Bourdieu approaches the field of education as an outsider. The French school system is structured in such a way as to dispose students from working class backgrounds (such as Bourdieu himself) to study for trades. There are exceptions, of course; Bourdieu's own success within the French school system was such that he was able to go on to study philosophy at the prestigious *Ecole normale superieure*, which provided him with the means and framework to pursue an academic career. Still, even though he has gone on to become Professor of Sociology at the *College de France*, perhaps the most prestigious French academic institution, Bourdieu has been always conscious of his difference from his colleagues. Indeed, he compares *Homo Academicus*, his study of the French intellectual field, to someone sitting in a zoo watching an exotic animal at play. Bourdieu's point is that while academics themselves are disposed to turn their inquiring gaze on other people, seeking to uncover the deeper structures and values that govern their lives, they are much more reluctant to turn this gaze upon themselves.

This chapter begins by discussing education's role as a field that shapes, and is shaped by, practices in other fields. We look at how the concept of habitus provides the core of Bourdieu's understanding of how schools work to reproduce social inequalities. We then consider how an understanding of the relations and forces that underpin school practice can assist students to negotiate this system successfully.

Education and social change

We can begin by identifying Bourdieu's position within one of the central debates in contemporary western societies. That is, is education the most effective mechanism for promoting social change and giving opportunities for less privileged groups to better themselves; or, on the contrary, does it tend to keep in place existing social divisions, and maintain the relative disadvantage of certain groups?

Bourdieu's position on this question is more complex than some writers have given him credit for. On the one hand, as a politically committed thinker he would like to see education transform social relations by providing opportunities for everyone; but on the other hand his various research projects have found that schools tend to have the function of reproducing social inequalities. This should not, however, lead to pessimism among those groups committed to using education as a vehicle for social change. Rather, Bourdieu's research helps us to see why education tends to reproduce social divisions, and therefore challenges all interested parties—educational bureaucrats, politicians, teachers, and of course students themselves—to make moves within the field that might bring about change.

Heteronomous and autonomous poles

As we pointed out in Chapter 5, Bourdieu not only divides the social space up into fields, but also suggests that the political field has a determining role, to a greater or lesser extent, on all other fields. And certainly, the political field has intervened directly into the educational field to provide a vision and direct its efforts. But it is not the only field that has the ability to interact with, and have an impact on, education. To develop this further, we need to look more closely at Bourdieu's concept of 'field', and particularly the distinction he draws between the autonomous pole of a field (that which tends to be isolated and removed from the rest of society) and the heteronomous pole of the same field (that which is bound up very closely in relations with the rest of society). Within the field of education, for instance, the autonomous pole would be associated with attitudes to education that are committed to learning for its own sake; or the view that the school is a space for nurturing the spiritual and intellectual growth of the child within a supportive environment. Films such as *Goodbye Mr Chips* and *To Sir With Love* extol this vision of schooling. It is a vision that is associated with a certain view of childhood as somehow a pure and pristine condition, uncorrupted by such 'threats' as sexuality, technology and market forces. At the heteronomous pole, by contrast, we might find questions about student fees and loans, the cost value of particular subjects, disciplines or even schools, and so on.

We can use this distinction between heteronomous and autonomous discourses to map the way in which heteronomous forces—those associated with economics and commoditisation—are increasingly impinging upon the field of schooling. This is because Bourdieu's 'double vision' recognises that all positions within a field, far from being static and complete unto themselves, are shaped by the tensions between autonomous and heteronomous forces. And it is apparent that heteronomous tendencies associated with the market are increasingly impacting on childhood itself and also on school systems in contemporary western societies. The idea that schools must pay their way, for instance, or that school success should be judged according to business models, accompanies an associated move in which children are exposed to advertising campaigns through a range of media, including the Internet. So on the one hand, governments, including that of France, are using terms and concepts like 'league tables', 'benchmarking', 'national testing' and 'quality control' to measure efficiency and productivity and demonstrate the extent of their commitment to a literally business-like approach to schooling. And on the other hand, businesses themselves are increasingly viewing children, and the concept of childhood, as a desirable market for toys, fashion and other commodities. In a sense, these two trends have the effect of producing children and their experiences as commodities; that is, things to be bought and sold on the market. We can go so far as to say that, from this perspective, a person's significance within the field of schooling has an inverse relationship with their autonomy. That is, if an educationalist ignores these market imperatives and seeks to maintain an autonomous approach to nurturing children's intellectual and spiritual growth, they are unlikely to have much authority or influence within the school system.

We should qualify this by recognising that the articulation of autonomous values still has a place within schooling, and that these values work to give schools a special and particular place and role within the social field. But while it is acceptable and indeed valuable to articulate a commitment to nurturing the child's whole growth as an individual, the 'real work' of schools largely takes place elsewhere, producing a 'student commodity' amenable to the interests of government, business and other heteronomous influences.

In practice, rather than being fixed to either the autonomous or heteronomous poles, teachers move between these extremes in order to negotiate the various forces and imperatives with which they are confronted. The degree to which a teacher is able and free to move between these poles, however, can be limited by their experiences and expectations (that is, their habitus).

Education and cultural capital

Given that Bourdieu regards social relations as intrinsic to practices within the field of education, he is vitally interested in identifying the social background of the various individuals who make up the field. For example, in some of his research into the French school system, Bourdieu considers the employment types of students' parents as a guide to their level of success within the school environment. Of course, there are numerous other ways of mapping an individual's social background: family income level, place of residence, religious affiliation, and so on. But for Bourdieu, employment types serve as a useful means of differentiating social groups into various classes. For example, teachers would be regarded as intellectual workers and identified as part of the knowledge class, while farm hands would be identified as rural workers and hence part of the labouring class.

Having identified various class groups, Bourdieu then proceeds to map relations between them in terms of their relative dominance and subordination. He does this on the basis of the relative amount of capital that each class group possesses. This capital could be economic, in terms of financial assets, but it could take other forms—for instance, the cultural capital associated with a university degree. The point about the various forms of capital is that they are recognised as having value and they can be traded or exchanged for desired outcomes within their own field or within others. Economic capital, say one hundred dollars, can be exchanged for a night at an expensive hotel. Cultural capital, such as a university degree, can be exchanged for a desired job. And if you have symbolic capital as an expert on Bourdieu, you may be able to cash in on this by agreeing to help your fellow students with an essay using his ideas only if they grant you certain favours in return.

Education is an important field because of its capacity to confer capital, particularly cultural capital, upon its participants. Indeed, education can be referred to as an academic market in terms of its distribution of such cultural capital. This capital can be measured in three forms: relating to individuals, to objects, and to institutions. Individuals are conferred with this capital through exhibiting an educated character, based on their knowledge, refined accents, dispositions to learn and value education highly, and so on. Objects such as books, qualifications and 'knowledge machines' such as computers are laden with cultural capital. And institutions such as libraries, elite schools and universities carry this form of capital.

The point about such cultural capital is that it plays a crucial role in the reproduction of dominant social relations and structures. Knowledge tends to be seen as a good in itself, but linking it to the concept of cultural capital helps us to see how it operates in terms of social inequality. Certain forms of knowledge, such as those associated with formal learning, are conferred with much more cultural capital than those forms of learning associated with practical activities like riding a bike. Because the cultural capital of knowledge is inequitably distributed, tending to favour those who occupy positions and dispositions that provide access to these socially legitimated and valued ways of knowing, knowledge becomes a marker of distinction and social privilege.

In France, this distribution of cultural capital has been regulated according to the particular structural characteristics of the school system, with the distinction made between elite *lycées* with their focus on academic excellence, and the colleges and elementary schools that have focused on more vocationally based education. The education system is also heavily centralised, so that the focus has tended to be more on standardising the curriculum than on taking account of the particular needs of different social groups. In this sense, French schools can be understood as factories of knowledge, committed to promoting the values of precise and analytical thought and elevated language, rather than as places for social interaction.

In texts such as *Reproduction in Education, Society and Culture, Academic Discourse* and *The State Nobility*, Bourdieu and his co-writers have unearthed a wealth of sociological data indicating how the education system within France has tended to reproduce these class positions. That is, the children of those who have occupied relatively privileged positions within the social class hierarchy have tended to ascend to similar positions, while the children of those who lack this privilege have tended to remain in relatively dominated positions. This is an important point about Bourdieu's work generally. His theoretical models have been developed in response to his surprise at finding the forces of reproduction so firmly established.

In this context, Bourdieu makes the point that the capital accrued from educational institutions only has value in fields that recognise and share this value. So it can be possible for people to lack the cultural capital of a school leaving certificate or university degree, but still succeed in other fields. A member of a circus family who has received little formal schooling, for example, may make up for this with the skills they have learnt on the road, and the circus tricks such as lion taming or acrobatics that have been passed on to them by their family. The phrase 'the university of life' captures this idea of the value of learning done in other than in formal educational settings.

The increasing tendency for western governments to view education as a principal means for alleviating social disadvantage, however, has meant that formal educational qualifications tend to be highly valued within more and more fields. It is difficult to succeed in many fields without the cultural capital such qualifications provide. The cultural capital bound up in a degree or certificate is increasingly mandatory for entry into the field of employment. In many countries, for example, it is necessary to have a qualification from a training college to be permitted to cut people's hair on a professional basis. Though a person may have a natural ability to cut hair and create wondrous follicle effects upon the heads of friends and family, unless they have an approved certificate from a training college, they are not qualified to be employed in a hairdressing salon. And while the circus performer mentioned above may be able to practise their skills in the circus ring, they may be restricted from taking on other tasks within the circus, such as doing maintenance and repairs on the trucks carrying the circusrig from town to town, unless they have an approved mechanic's certificate from a recognised training institution.

This incursion of education into other fields has tended to encourage more and more students to stay on in school and go on to university or college. This trend then creates a momentum (some would say a vicious circle) in which formal education is accorded greater value within the society at large, and at the same time, and as a result, has a greater capacity to determine how much value each member of that society possesses. It is in this context that we can see why the Blair Labour government in Britain might regard 'education, education, education' as the key to people achieving a better life for themselves and their families. That is why Bourdieu's research findings and his theories for explaining them have such importance.

Theories of school and social reproduction

We can now return to Bourdieu's case that, rather than promoting social change, educational institutions such as schools tend to reproduce existing social relations and inequalities. Of course this is not only Bourdieu's argument; his studies can be compared with contemporary theorists such as Samuel Bowles and Herbet Gintis, who have considered how structures of capitalism impose themselves on educational opportunities within an American context, and Bob Connell, who has considered how ruling class values have informed schooling within Australia. Indeed, it is worth considering Bourdieu's case in comparison with other theories about why schools maintain social disadvantage. One theory, which might be called a traditional Marxist view, is that members of the ruling class have a vested interest in maintaining their domination, and that they do this by limiting the opportunities for members of less powerful groups to have access to educational resources. According to this theory, it is access to economic capital that directly determines how much value the school experience will be. For example, a member of a well-off family is likely to be able to afford to attend a private school where there are all the most up-to-date technological facilities; where she will have access to tutorial support if she is having problems with any of her subjects; where she is assisted at developing her skills in extra-curricular areas such as dance and origami; and where she can tap into lifelong learning networks with like-minded individuals—'the old school tie' effect. A child from a less prosperous family, on the other hand, may be forced to attend a poorly funded state-run school where the technological aids are years out of date and falling to bits; where the teachers may be too harried by the effort of managing large classes of unruly students to be able to offer anything but the most cursory help; and where the extra-curricular activities are more likely to involve fighting and smoking than origami.

A second theory, which might be identified as a hegemonic view of schooling, suggests that the role of schools is to make students believe that the existing social relations are just and natural and in their interests. This theory would encourage students to believe that some of their peers achieve higher results because they work harder or are naturally good at those subjects. It may encourage low achieving students to believe that they are just not 'cut out' for school and that they can compensate by pursuing opportunities in other areas, such as sport.

Other theorists make the point that teachers and educational bureaucrats tend to come from fairly privileged social backgrounds, and are disposed to favour students who share their values and attitudes. A child from a background similar to that of her teachers will not have to make a big adjustment to school; she will tend to find the attitudes of teachers (their emphasis on 'good' manners, their tendency to encourage quiet reading) almost exactly the same as her parents at home. So when a child feels at home at school, this is likely to be because the school bears sufficient resemblance to home to provide that sense of security. A child from a family where the parents have low-paid labouring jobs will be likely to find school a very alien and hostile environment. This child may not have an understanding of what the educational institution promotes as the 'good' manners that he is expected to display, or have had any previous experience of quiet reading at home.

A related view is that the types of language (or discourse) that schools use to educate students tend to favour those who are already exposed to this type of language at home. Studies, such as those conducted by the British linguist Basil Bernstein, have found that middle- and working-class families tend to have very different vocabularies, and ways of phrasing and expressing their ideas. Again, a child from a less privileged family is likely to find the language used both in the formal classes, and outside class in situations like the morning assembly, very different from that to which she is accustomed at home. School, from this perspective, means acquiring a foreign language which certain students have already mastered.

Educational habitus

Bourdieu would not fundamentally disagree with any of these theories for the school system as an agent of social reproduction. He recognises that economic capital has a significant impact on access to educational resources. He would also note that while schools tend to encourage a belief that they serve the children's interests, they are really disposed to serving the interests of children who have already had access to the kind of values and environment which the school system promotes, at least partly through the kind of discourses that it employs.

Where Bourdieu can be distinguished from these theoretical perspectives is in his conception of the mechanism that educational systems employ to reproduce existing social relations in students. For Bourdieu it is the habitus that is the key. The habitus is the set of durable dispositions that people carry within them that shapes their attitudes, behaviours and responses to given situations. The point is that the habitus is not found just at the level of people's thoughts (their consciousness), nor just in the language they use, though these are important dimensions of it. The habitus also works at the level of the body, shaping what might seem its instinctive responses; and it is as much unconscious as conscious. For example, when a student goes from one class to the next, she is generally not conscious of the path she follows (she's done it countless times before), but is on 'automatic pilot'. The habitus expresses itself in the innumerable mundane practices such as walking between classes that make up everyday life.

Just as the habitus is not found necessarily at the level of consciousness, so too—in contrast to the Marxist perspective—it is not directly determined by economic relations. Rather, it is a complex array of strategies and tactics that work to provide people with the best available outcome, given the circumstances they are facing. So the path our student takes will perhaps allow her to move between one class and the next in the shortest possible time; alternatively, it may not offer the shortest trip but affords her a pleasant view of some gardens; or it allows her to avoid someone whom she does not like. We can also see how a student's habitus impacts on the way she approaches homework: where, when and how it is done or not done within the widely varying home environment.

And, as we noted in Chapter 5, the habitus does not only apply to the individual, but has a collective aspect. Each student is different in that they have had personal experiences that have fashioned their attitudes and values. In addition, each person has a different physical character, based on genetic development, diet, personal experience and so forth. But at the same time, the habitus is collective in the sense that the common situation in which students find themselves disposes them to certain shared actions: taking exams, entering classrooms, writing assignments and so forth.

For Bourdieu it is through the habitus that social reproduction takes place. We discussed earlier how education, like any field, is comprised of complex objective relations and structures. These include the relations between teachers, students and the subject matter of the various disciplines to which they are

115

exposed; the bureaucratic structure of the school and its relations with other schools and state agencies that support it; the class relations that pertain between different students, or between students and teachers, and so on. It is evident that these structures and relations are complex and dynamic. They are never fully in place once and for all, but are subject to shifts and movements within the field itself. Bourdieu's point is that these structures and relations do not exist 'out there', removed from the individuals, but rather that they are embodied, absorbed into the sense making apparatus of the individual in order to constitute the practical reason of the habitus.

The habitus is thus the means through which the values and relations of the school are inculcated and reproduced within the child. The child will take to school the habitus they have acquired in their early years within the home, and that habitus will be acted on by their experiences at school. So, for Bourdieu, home and family life also play a significant role in social reproduction, as the degree to which the child's family habitus fits in with the school habitus has consequences for the success of the child in acquiring the values, dispositions and cultural capital that characterise the school.

Educational discourse

One of the most effective instruments for accomplishing this process of embodiment, according to Bourdieu, is language. That is why mastering each academic subject depends on coming to terms with its language (that is, discourse). Beyond the subject matter, all the complex and routine relations that characterise the day-to-day operations of the school are communicated through various forms of discourse: the letter from a parent explaining why a child has been away; the address from the principal to the student body; the inspirational talk from the swimming coach to the team before they go out to compete. And just as objective relations are structured around relatively dominant or dominated positions, so too language operates as a system of relations that helps reproduce these dominant and dominated positions. When teachers—as they routinely do—distinguish between proper and improper language use, or between elegant phrasing and crude expression, they are making these distinctions.

For Bourdieu the habitus is a cultural agent before it is a social form of identity. By this he means that it is cultural practices that shape, determine and help reproduce social relations. We can relate this idea to the concept of the 'cultural arbitrary', a term Bourdieu uses to suggest that the different power relations that pertain in our culture have no necessary basis. That is, they are not tied to some reality beyond themselves, such as some biological law. This means the basis of these divisions exists in some culturally arbitrary or symbolic realm, such as language or images.

Cultural arbitrary and symbolic violence

The film *The Lion King* (1994) can be used as an example of how the cultural arbitrary relates to symbolic violence and the role of pedagogic action, both important elements of educational practice. The divisions and different power relations between the animals in *The Lion King* are presented not as being arbitrary, but as tied to a biological reference point, the circle of life. According to the circle of life, everything is connected in the food chain, creating a hierarchy leading up to the lions, who are the kings of the jungle. But if we step back and reflect that *The Lion King* is actually a popular Hollywood film aimed at children, we can see that it functions as a form of symbolic violence. The film works through its narrative to encourage or dispose viewers to make a connection between the divisions that apply in the animal 'kingdom', and the social divisions that apply in their own culture.

An early scene shows the young lion, Simba, entering the cave where his parents are shown sleeping side by side, and encouraging his father to get up and play with him. The viewer is disposed to connect this scene with their own lives in which jumping on parents' beds to get them up is a fairly regular

117

occurrence (at least for young viewers). Simba's father, Mufasa, performs a customary paternal and pedagogic role by teaching his son the ways of the world as they sit outside the cave looking at their kingdom laid out before them. He does this by making the different power positions occupied by the animals seem natural and necessary, and by distinguishing the places 'touched by the sun', which constitute the lions' privileged domain, from the dark, shadowy world beyond, which Simba finds to be a haven for hyenas, who are presented as untrustworthy and devious animals.

Again, a reading of Bourdieu enables us to make connections with our culture, constituted as it is by different positions within social hierarchies that can be understood in terms of their relative dominance. When the arbitrary nature of these hierarchies is disguised by making connections with a world where the divisions are presented as necessary and vital to the 'health' of that culture, as occurs in *The Lion King*, a form of symbolic violence is being enacted. The violence is symbolic because it is not directly physical, but its effect is just as significant because it enables certain groups occupying privileged positions to maintain dominance over others. In this case, it enables the lions to justify to themselves their tendency to eat the antelopes. So symbolic violence plays a fundamental role in the reproduction and naturalising of the social hierarchy.

Pedagogic action

For Bourdieu, a principal form of symbolic violence is pedagogic action, or teaching the ways of the world, as Mufasa does to Simba. In contemporary western societies, such pedagogic action is less the role of parents and more the responsibility of schools. Indeed it is because the power relations that pertain in society are arbitrary and not natural and necessary that they require some sort of pedagogic action in order to be learned and absorbed.

Pedagogic action proceeds by promoting certain *doxa* and consecrating certain positions and (life) styles. Doxa, as we discussed in earlier chapters, can be understood as regimes of truth or forms of social orthodoxy. These are, typically, articulated by bodies of knowledge that perform this sort of 'reproductive' function by communicating the values and meanings of the existing social order, values that students are disposed to accept as natural and legitimate. Bourdieu calls this acceptance 'misrecognition', because it fails to recognise or engage with the arbitrary nature of social divisions and differential relations of power. Rather, students come to accept these divisions and relations as second nature, in the same way that it becomes second nature to butter bread or throw a baseball—once a knowledge or skill is acquired, it is not something that needs to be thought about or reflected on to any great extent.

Doxa works to distinguish the thinkable from the unthinkable, so that certain courses of action, those that seriously challenge established social relations, become literally unthinkable—or at least, inarticulable. For example, societies such as the United States and Australia were formed on the basis of forcibly removing indigenous people from their lands, an injustice that is increasingly being recognised. Yet it would be unthinkable that Native Americans and Aborigines would be given all their territories back and everyone else would pack up and go back to Europe or somewhere else.

Similarly, in contemporary western societies, it would be unthinkable for education to be taken out of the hands of the schools and educational bureaucracies and given back wholly to the parents. For the work of reproduction through doxa to be accomplished, the role of the parents (especially those from relatively powerless social positions) within the educational field needs to be kept strictly limited.

Accordingly, the field of education assumes this role and through various measures (limiting access of parents to the school, requiring parents to come to the school rather than requiring that the school should go out into the domain of the parents, requiring that the parent should read and sign report cards that the school has authorised, and so forth) the parents' relatively powerless position is affirmed and reproduced. When parents are required to sign students' report cards, the school is showing that it is monitoring not only the performance of students, but also that of parents in terms of how much support they are providing for the school institution's pedagogic action.

We can see an example of the school system's power over parents in the following examples of parents' notes to teachers taken from Texas:

> Please excuse Gloria from Jim today. She is
> administrating.
> Please excuse Roland from P.E. for a few days. Yesterday he
> fell out of a tree and misplaced his hip.
> John has been absent because he had two teeth taken out of
> his face.
> Carlos was absent yesterday because he was
> playing football. He was hurt in the growing part.
> Megan could not come to school today because she has been
> bothered by very close veins.

The parents' evident failure to master a medical and health discourse becomes a source of humour. But it is noteworthy that these parents feel they need to attempt to master a discourse that is clearly alien to them, but which would be familiar to school officials. In other words, the parents feel the need to communicate with the school on its terms rather than their own.

Doxa also works to distinguish the thinkable from the unthinkable in terms of students' aspirations. For the habitus created by, and through, the doxa includes an awareness of the very restricted options available for students in terms of their own cultural trajectory. A student from a family which is relatively impoverished in terms of economic and cultural capital, and who accordingly occupies a relatively low position on the social hierarchy, will unconsciously accept that certain options and pathways, such as going to an 'elite' university or becoming a concert pianist, will not be open for her. Such options become unthinkable.

Similarly, despite a generation of affirmative action in schools and in society more generally, many girls in western societies still routinely opt for subjects that they see as suited to their gender: art, domestic science, and humanities subjects such as history and languages. While certain people see this trend as related to 'natural' differences between the sexes, Bourdieu's approach relates it to the role of doxa in reproducing the cultural arbitrary.

Consecration

Working in with doxa to make these distinctions is the practice of consecration. For Bourdieu, certain positions and lifestyles produced through pedagogical action become consecrated, or endowed with a special aura and distinction denied other practices. For example, a child who exhibits a musical genius such that she is able to master the works of Beethoven and Mozart by the age of eleven will be granted this consecrated position. This will be marked by the investment of considerable cultural capital—awards and trophies, invitations to perform before presidents and royalty—and less considerable economic capital (such consecrated positions are deemed to be separate from, and above, the murky world of money). The educational field facilitates this process of consecration by providing certain support and pathways for the musical genius. These may include master-classes from a famous concert pianist, bursaries to travel overseas and study under the tuition of an expert in this field, and scholarships that would allow the student to go to a conservatorium of music.

It is unlikely that such support would be available for a student whose musical inclination involved ritualistically destroying property with a guitar in the manner of a heavy metal group. This accomplishment would tend to take place away from the school institution, perhaps in the garage at home. Indeed such an ability would be as likely to have the school regard the student as 'delinquent' and 'threatening', rather than as gifted and talented. Her cultural trajectory would be likely to be removed from the education field, and dispose her to form a band that plays the club and pub circuit, gain an agent and a deal with a record company, and perhaps aim to produce a video clip and appear on MTV.

Who and what gets consecrated within the educational field is, however, open to transformation. An example is the experience of Paul McCartney, bass player and songwriter with the Beatles. The cultural trajectory followed by the Beatles, in its formative stages, was very much like our heavy metal player. Far from having his interest in guitar playing sanctioned by the educational field, Paul McCartney used to play truant from his school to practise chords with John Lennon. The band gained its foothold through playing in fairly 'rough and ready' venues in Liverpool such as the Cavern, and strip clubs in Hamburg, before securing themselves a manager and a record contract with EMI. Yet it is interesting that in an interview with Michael Parkinson on BBC television, Paul suggested that the Beatles felt they had the edge on other bands because of their level of education; Paul and George attended a grammar school, while John went to art college. Thus, even though educational institutions were very much removed from the world of rock and roll music, educational advantage was still perceived to constitute some form of capital within this world.

In the 1990s, having won fame and fortune, Paul McCartney donated a lot of money to establishing the Liverpool Institute of Performing Arts, designed to provide support and training for talented performers, including those who prefer the medium of rock and roll music. This donation is believed to be partly responsible for Paul McCartney being awarded a knighthood in 1997, thus confirming his own consecrated position within the British establishment. While the idea of students actually 'learning' how to do rock and roll music in established educational institutions such as a conservatorium of music is still somewhat scandalous, for some people at least it is acceptable, and figures like Paul McCartney, who possess considerable cultural and economic capital, can bring about transformations within the field.

For Bourdieu, then, the role of the education field generally, and the school system within it, is to promote the objective interests of the dominant class. These interests can be summarised as maintaining a cultural space characterised by social hierarchies and division, and differential relations of power secured through the uneven distribution of economic and cultural capital throughout positions that make up this cultural space.

Delinquency and deviance

It is not surprising then that many students feel disposed to rebel against the pressures to reproduce that schools place upon them. Students from non-privileged backgrounds—as well as their families—may feel that the values and language styles that they are accustomed to use at home are in danger of being lost. In this sense, the school experience can be one in which their backgrounds are devalued. Students from more privileged backgrounds might also find the school system stifling their individuality. The film *Dead Poets Society*, for instance, showed how a privileged student's attempts to challenge school and parental authority (by appearing in a play when he had been forbidden to do so by his father, on the grounds that theatre is frivolous) led to his destruction.

For Bourdieu these failures, as marked by rebellious students or high rates of attrition, are already anticipated by the school system. In reproducing the social relations of the wider world, schools need to be able to distinguish between the good and the bad, the 'model' students from the delinquents. Much of the 'real work' of schools consists of making these distinctions. This is why certain students feel disposed to devote much of their school time not to the formal curriculum, but to participating as a member of a group or 'gang' acting out mild or extreme versions of delinquent behaviour: swearing, smoking, sex, taking drugs and so forth. It is also evident in the way a student body routinely feels disposed to identify themselves (or other students) within a particular category: jocks, geeks, surfies, nerds, space cadets and so forth. So while being a member of a gang that engages in rebellious behaviour might give 'Nostril Ned' a certain value and cultural capital within that setting, this rebelliousness also operates to confirm Ned in a dominated (relatively powerless) position of being a delinquent within the society as a whole. One of the prime roles of schools, then, is to identify and manage social deviancy of the sort Ned and his cohorts engage in.

Part of this deviancy is expressed as an adolescent sub-culture which, in its language, dress and modes of behaviour, is consciously at odds with the cultivated official culture of the school. When representatives of the official school culture attempt to bridge this gap by dressing in a 'cool' manner, or self-consciously using adolescent argot such as 'going off', they are likely to be treated with disdain by both the school and its rebellious students. This is because they have breached the rules of the game in failing to maintain the distinction between the proper and the improper school culture. In a sense the success of the school experience depends upon this failure to communicate across this cultural gap.

We can take this point further to suggest that the capacity to be empowered tends to be confined to those who are in some sense empowered already. For example, one of the most celebrated mechanisms for empowering school students in terms of their conception of themselves and their abilities is music, as films like *Mr Holland's Opus* have indicated. Yet this sense of empowerment through music tends to be confined to those students who have access to musical instruments, the opportunity for extra tuition, a home environment disposed to regard musical expression as valuable, and a confidence and social ease with performing in front of people in auditoria and theatres. Students from underprivileged backgrounds, without access to these instruments of empowerment, are implicitly being trained to (mis)recognise their options in life as not including the world of musical performance.

In making these distinctions, schools are actively engaged in distributing value and conferring relative degrees of cultural capital upon the students. While such educational capital tends to determine a person's success in the wider world, this is not always the case. We often hear stories of a famous sports player or rock musician who can remember being told by a teacher that they should spend less time on their favoured activity, because it will not get them far in life. Again, this shows that while there tends to be a general fit between the forms of distinction and kinds of cultural capital promoted in school and those that apply in the wider world, this is not entirely the case, and there are gaps between the two.

It is in relation to these gaps that we can return to the point made by Bourdieu at the beginning of this chapter. Although he is often regarded as a pessimist in the way he regards the school system as being more an agent of social reproduction rather than transformation, he might rather be seen as being provisionally optimistic. First, in recognising how objective relations become embodied in students through the discourses and everyday practices of schools, he offers a way of understanding not just what schools do to students, but how they do it. Second, his conception of habitus recognises some gap between objective relations and subjective practices. A model student may have to play the game, by accepting the rules and following the moves the school system lays down, but there are certain hidden and secret tactics that she can adopt to distance herself from the system, to gain some space apart for herself. These may range from daydreaming during the distinguished invited guest's speech day address to responding to a survey questionnaire that asks for general comments on a particular subject: 'Elephants are large grey animals with trunks. This is a very general comment and might vary with individual cases'. In opposition to Ned's rebelliousness, that results in him being labelled a delinquent, this student practises a more discreet and secretive way of distinguishing herself from the play of the system.

Conclusion

This chapter has shown how Bourdieu's theories recognise schools as being principal agents of social reproduction. The key features for Bourdieu are:

- How the habitus, as a set of durable dispositions, is shaped by, and helps shape, pedagogical action within the school.
- How students can use a reflective understanding of the way in which objective relations underpin school operations in order to negotiate these relations.

The next chapter engages further with Bourdieu's ideas on the field of education, focusing specifically on the tertiary sector.

Further reading

Bourdieu, Pierre 1973, 'Cultural reproduction and social reproduction', in Richard Brown ed., *Knowledge, Education and Cultural Change: Papers in the Sociology of Education*, Tavistock, London, pp. 71–112

Grenfell, Michael and David James with Philip Hodkinson, Diane Reay and Derek Robbins 1998, *Bourdieu and Education: Acts of Practical Theory*, Falmer Press, London.

Nash, Roy 1999, 'Bourdieu, "Habitus", and educational research: is it all worth the candle?' *British Journal of Sociology of Education*, 20, 2, June, pp. 175–87

7

Bourdieu and higher education

The previous chapter considered the implications of Bourdieu's ideas for secondary school education. In this chapter the focus is on higher education, such as the university system derived from western Europe (which applies in much of the rest of the world), and the college system within the United States. In some ways higher education marks a continuation of the practices of secondary education, while in other ways it represents quite a marked shift.

While Bourdieu has written extensively on the higher education system, generally he has confined his comments to the French system. Nevertheless, we can see similar trends, to a greater or lesser extent, applying within other higher education systems throughout the world. Bourdieu's discussion of the French higher education system can be found in books such as *Academic Discourse* (1992c), *Homo Academicus* (1988), *The State Nobility* (1996a), *Practical Reason* (1998d) and *Pascalian Meditations* (2000) as well as in a large number of articles. Indeed, in some of the lectures delivered to foreign audiences that appear in *Practical Reason*, Bourdieu is at pains to show how his work has relevance for all social systems, not just France.

This chapter will discuss how the higher education system establishes structural relations between teachers and students that help to maintain the distinction between one and the other. It also considers the different positions and dispositions of various academic disciplines, and goes on to consider the roles of the scholastic point of view in equipping students with a set of literacies that assist them in negotiating the academic field, and producing themselves as marketable commodities.

Secondary and higher education

For Bourdieu, the higher education system resembles the school system in its work to 'consecrate' social distinctions by cultivating certain ways of acting that have the effect of reproducing social inequality. Even though more and more people in western societies now have the opportunity to attend university, the system as a whole continues to work to reinforce privilege. This is done in a myriad of ways, such as making distinctions between elite universities (such as Oxford and Yale) and less prestigious centres of higher education (such as polytechnic colleges); and by consecrating certain ways of acting within the university (the ability to write elegantly, the capacity to exhibit an 'effortless superiority' in one's dealing with others and so on). If we think of the image of the scholar walking among the dreaming spires of Oxford, for example, we can recognise how higher education produces that air of distinction vital to the reproduction of social division. Television series such as *Brideshead Revisited*, which followed the experiences of an upper-class British family (in and out of university), and *Inspector Morse*, which features a highly educated police inspector, help to make this image well-known and recognised. It is in this way that it becomes consecrated.

One important difference, however, is that while schools are primarily concerned with the transmission of knowledge, universities are as much concerned with the production of knowledge. This is why in most universities, and particularly the elite ones, teaching is accorded much less importance than research and publications. If schools, through the transmission of knowledge, act as agents of reproduction, universities produce the forms of knowledge that help make the objective relations into which people are reproduced.

Objectification through forms of knowledge

In making this point, Bourdieu is arguing against the idea that the development of knowledge is simply a noble cause that allows us to gain progressively greater understanding of, and control over, the world in which we live. Rather, Bourdieu is concerned with the way in which knowledge forms contribute to the objective relations and social divisions which underlie our everyday lives. So knowledge is always 'interested'; it is always tied up with questions of social power.

We saw in Chapter 6 that schools tended to be concerned with maintaining some degree of distance between their practices and those of students. One of the ways they do this is through the identification of a class of delinquent students, or 'outsiders'. Similarly, even though entry to higher education indicates students have successfully managed the passage through schools—generating and maintaining a distance between academic staff and students is a fundamental part of university practice.

One of the ways in which universities maintain their distance from students is through the use of rituals, such as the processions of staff in their academic gowns. These processions need to be taken very seriously, even—perhaps especially—when it is difficult to do so. One Australian university has designed its academic gown around the colours of the university emblem, a rosella. Even though this means that privileged staff attend dignified academic ceremonies dressed as uncommonly large tropical birds, their status as fit and proper members of the community is rarely in question (at least as far as they are concerned). On the contrary, this dress serves to establish their high status within that particular university community.

This distance will vary from country to country. For example, a Canadian lecturer who taught on exchange at an Australian university remarked that one of the hardest adjustments he had to make was getting used to students calling him by his first name. On the other hand, many elite universities still conduct classes in which the tutor refers to class members by their surnames: 'Miss Jones', 'Mr Fowler' and so forth. An extreme form of this distinction between lecturer and class was found in the person of Arthur Quiller Couch, Professor of English at Cambridge University during the early years of the twentieth century, who would begin lectures by addressing the class as 'Gentlemen', even though they largely consisted of women (Eagleton 1983: 28).

A second way in which universities generate distance between lecturer and students is through the layout of the built environment of the institution. For example, one of the principal forms of university teaching, the lecture, tends to involve the lecturer delivering a monologue from behind a lectern on a podium in front of a large hall seating hundreds of students. It serves to confirm that the lecturer is removed from, and operates on, a different, more elevated level than students.

A third and related way of maintaining distance is through the kind of language (academic discourse) that university teachers employ. Academic discourse is a specialised language that confers distinction and value (that is, cultural capital) upon those who employ it. In one sense, it is the business of universities to ground students in academic discourse; or, more specifically, in the discourse of the particular academic discipline they are studying. But unlike schools, which explicitly train students in how to use the officially valued discourses, teaching them how to use 'standard' English and make 'correct' use of grammar, universities tend to work more implicitly. It is almost assumed that good students will master this mysterious academic discourse without being told (or needing to be told) how to do so. Thus, rather than lecturers seeking to 'reach' students by speaking on the same level as them, the 'good' university lecturer is expected to deliver an elegant and erudite oratory, full of flowery metaphors, obscure allusions, French and Latin tags and so forth. All of this is designed to communicate the lecturer's mastery or effortless superiority over the students, so that learning proceeds through a kind of osmosis. Of course, it might be objected here that Bourdieu's argument, drawn as it is from the particular conditions pertaining in the French higher education system, is simply too negative, and fails to recognise the genuine attempts of certain higher education institutions and their teachers to help students master academic discourse. Certainly, we should allow that there are such procedures. We can make the point, however, that the legitimated or consecrated academic disciplines tend to be couched in a specialised and esoteric language, the access to which distinguishes lecturers from their students.

For Bourdieu, higher education tends to involve a series of games in which lecturers and students are complicit, that are designed to show that the transmission of knowledge is actually taking place. Whether it really is or not is another matter. It is significant, in this context, that so many universities still rely on the traditional lecture method for transmitting knowledge. This is in spite of the fact that the student could easily access the information in the lecture from other sites, such as a book or a web page. Yet still the university invests in the game (or pretence) that the lecture involves the sharing of a secret and special knowledge between lecturer and student.

Through such ritualised games as the lecture, the university teacher speaks from the position of a distinguished club whose membership the student desires to join. The price of this membership is measured in the cultural capital the students are able to generate through immersing themselves in the sacred texts and learned discourse of that academic discipline. They will then reproduce this learned discourse in their essays, aiming for that effortless mastery of language that distinguishes the good student.

Of course not all students are able to exhibit such mastery. Indeed this failure (which most students display to a greater or lesser extent) lies at the heart of the higher educational system: students are charged with reproducing a discourse that is foreign to them, but which they understand is important in negotiating their way through their university careers. Accordingly, a typical university student will pick up certain key words and phrases which they either find their teachers routinely using, or see cropping up again and again in the research that they undertake in preparation for assignments. They will feel it important to include these terms in their essays, even though their understanding of them may be astray. Often the 'howlers' or glaring errors that occur in student essays and which provide great amusement to university examiners are the result of this inability to master an unfamiliar language. Examiners may well collect these howlers to help keep them sane during long bouts of marking; however, it is also a way of confirming their superiority to students in terms of their own mastery of their relevant academic discourse. They are able to distinguish their comfort with, and control over, these terms from their students' evident discomfort.

These rituals continue even as students ascend the academic ladder. In *Homo Academicus*, Bourdieu discusses the way in which graduate students attach themselves to favoured professors as a way of progressing their career. In response, these professors are able to exercise their patronage in such a way that confirms their power, for example by controlling the time the student has to take before their thesis might be considered suitable for examination.

Mapping disciplines within the higher education field

Within the higher education field, different disciplines have different functions and therefore enjoy differential relations to authority. While the education field, like all others, is overdetermined by the political field, certain disciplines are more centrally located in terms of this relationship. In the French higher education field, for example, Bourdieu finds that the disciplines of law, medicine and theology have a specially privileged relationship to the political field and, therefore, to lines of authority within the university. This is because these disciplines act as agents of reproduction for social authorities: law administers the social body's legal system; medicine administers the social body's physical health; theology tends the social body's moral wellbeing. Bourdieu's research finds that the students entering these fields are far more likely to be the offspring of privileged parents than are students who enter other academic disciplines such as education or applied science. These fields also tend to facilitate access to other powerful fields. For example, a number of people who have an academic background in law have attained influential positions within the political field, such as the former American president Bill Clinton, or British prime minister Tony Blair. In other western higher education systems, the disciplines of business and information technology seem to have this status. They are the ones that are valued by powerful economic and political forces as disciplines which, because they are imbued with the values of financial management and technology, work in with the interests increasingly shaping education and other fields within these societies.

Those disciplines that do not have this sort of access to social authority have to find other ways of validating themselves and claiming legitimation. In certain instances, the very lack of social capital or interest becomes the means of staking claims for such legitimation. Disciplines such as philosophy, 'pure' science and higher mathematics make a virtue of the fact that they are perceived to be removed from the social world, claiming theirs is a 'disinterested' quest for higher truths and pure knowledge, unsullied by questions of political belief, social favour or economic gain. For example, certain scientists will tend to say that their discipline is 'value free'. This claim suggests that science is merely interested in finding the truth to problems such as splitting the atom or finding out the fundamental laws of the universe, and is not corrupted by issues of personal interest, political values or belief.

In a similar way disciplines in the humanities may claim that they are just concerned with promoting aesthetic values, finding the highest and purest form of human expression in areas such as fine art, music, drama and so forth. They are following the Romantic poet John Keats' dictum, taken from the poem 'Ode on a Grecian Urn', that: 'Beauty is truth, truth beauty,—that is all/Ye know on earth, and all ye need to know'. We can say then that while disciplines such as law, theology, medicine, business and information technology have a heteronomous relationship with other fields, and especially the field of power, disciplines such as pure science and fine arts, which seem removed from the rest of society and work according to their own internal rules and procedures, possess more of an autonomous status.

These latter disciplines work to position the university as a whole as some kind of 'ivory tower', removed from the rest of society. Indeed, this perception that the university is removed from immediate social relevance is what gives it its power and prestige. The university is regarded as some kind of sanctuary, in which students can come and reflect upon the larger questions of life, the universe and everything, free from the interference of the outside world. The university provides them with a space and also a time away from the immediate concerns of having to act in the social world.

In *Pascalian Mediations*, Bourdieu discusses this 'space' in terms of *skholé*, the notion of free time, which he sees as the condition of existence of all scholarly fields. Free time away from the hurried world of work disposes those who possess it towards a particular contemplative outlook on life that Bourdieu calls the scholastic disposition. He also points to the phenomenon of 'scholastic enclosure', where universities such as Cambridge and Harvard become cut off from the outside world. It is from this position that scholarly fields form a particular representation of the world that take it as an object of knowledge, something that can be represented in its entirety. It also means that disciplines like philosophy, which when practised in ancient Athens by people like Socrates was geared towards practical concerns, come to be located within the scholastic enclosure of the academy and removed from social life.

Certain university figures embody this sense of disconnectedness in their habitus, their everyday behaviours. The image of the mad scientist, with wild unruly hair, big spectacles and curious dress sense is an example of this. Another stereotype is of the humanities professor, who might dress in a very flamboyant style with cravat, brightly coloured waistcoat and striped trousers, and drop learned Latin quotations while strolling about the campus. The university field not only tolerates this eccentric behaviour; in a sense it disposes professors to it as a means of acting out an otherworldly habitus.

An example of the way in which the academic habitus disposes people to eccentric behaviour is a reputedly true story concerning the philosopher, Ludwig Wittgenstein. One day Wittgenstein was so distracted by the complexities of an issue he was working on that he strolled into the middle of a flower bed without realising it. When a gardener asked him what he was doing there, Wittgenstein replied: 'What are any of us doing here?' Of course, Bourdieu rejects this notion of certain intellectuals being above and beyond the social world. In other words, he recognises this view as being part of the process of misrecognition that the academic habitus instils in its practitioners. He points out that such a claim is one way in which such academics are able to gain a relatively privileged status within the wider social space, able to dictate the terms on which they are evaluated within that sphere. For example, if someone occupying a less privileged position, say as an unemployed greenkeeper, decided to devote his time to a consideration of the different variations in combinations of fish and chips, he would be regarded as a work-shy lunatic. Yet if someone occupying a privileged position within the university decided to devote his time to researching an obscure Victorian cross-dressing poet, this would probably be regarded as legitimate research.

These academics perform the socially important role of practising and embodying distinction. That is, they comprise a group who are valued for their role in expressing the higher values of refinement and effortless superiority. For Bourdieu, this status has the significant social function of naturalising the privilege and dominance of certain groups in a community. That is, distinction operates to reproduce the cultural arbitrary.

Academics occupy an ambiguous role in the cultural arbitrary because they might be identified as a dominated faction within a dominant group. They are dominated in the sense that they are subservient to those figures who have greater access to social and economic capital such as big business executives, politicians, lawyers, doctors and theologians. On the other hand, as university figures they carry considerable cultural capital and, accordingly, still form part of the dominant group and perform the important role of maintaining its distinction from other classes.

Sociology

In mapping various disciplines throughout the university field in this way, Bourdieu is both reinforcing and critiquing his position as a professor of sociology. Sociology, like the humanities and physical sciences, lacks the privileged access to social authority enjoyed by medicine, law and theology. Yet its position in respect of this dominated faction is also uncertain. As a social science, committed to applying scientific principles to the study of social institutions, sociology lacks the claims to a 'pure' rational vision of the physical sciences, while it is also unable to make the disinterested aesthetic claims that characterise the Humanities.

For Bourdieu, it is this position of being at odds with other disciplines that gives sociology its particular power. On the one hand, it can draw upon the objectifying methods of science to trace through structural relations that constitute positions within the social world. On the other hand, it can afford to be (and is disposed to be) open about its interests, its 'situatedness' within the circuits of power—not only within the university field of which it is a part, but also within the social world that it takes as the object of its study. Sociology, then, for Bourdieu—as we discussed in Chapter 4—offers not a pure scientific gaze but an interested one.

It is significant in this context that Bourdieu relates the rise of sociology within the French university system to the student protests and upheaval within this system in 1968. He identifies this as a moment when the questioning of the authority and claims of various pure and socially sanctioned disciplines could find expression in new disciplinary movements such as sociology. We could respond to these claims for sociology with the Mandy Rice Davies line: 'Well, he would say that, wouldn't he?' Given that he is open about his own position and its interests, reading Bourdieu as Bourdieu would suggest he ought to be read means that he has to make claims for sociology as some kind of privileged discipline.

The point we would like to make is that Bourdieu's ideas need not simply stay confined to sociology, but can serve as a more general way of seeing and working through the higher education system. In this context, it is significant that Bourdieu's work has been picked up and incorporated into disciplines throughout the academy. It has shaped social science disciplines such as education, politics and economics; found its way into emerging disciplines such as cultural studies; helped to reconstitute the terms of reference in established humanities disciplines such as history, philosophy and language study; and also been absorbed into the socially consecrated disciplines such as law. It is important to point out, however, that the movement of these ideas into other disciplines has not been easy or straightforward, and has often met with considerable resistance. This resistance works to position Bourdieu as an outsider, who is not bound by, and indeed threatens, the values and accepted procedures of that discipline. Such a status accords him and his ideas a particular force and cultural and symbolic capital. (It can be useful to have the reputation as a rebel, as this will attract those similarly disposed.)

Universalisation

This movement of Bourdieu's ideas across the academy can be related to what he sees as the universalising tendency of this higher educational field. We discussed above how the traditional university seemed removed, both in a temporal and spatial way, from the social world. Students and professors are given a vantage point to see the world from a larger and wider perspective than that available to those who are preoccupied with acting within it according to immediate demands and necessities. It is rather like a person who looks at a town from an overlooking hill, able to peer down at all the streets and houses. In some senses that person's perspective is more privileged than that of someone driving a car within the town, who is preoccupied with the immediate needs of negotiating the traffic and avoiding a crash. The spectator on the hill is granted the semblance of the objective perspective which Bourdieu sees as vital to reflexive practice. They are able to discern the structural relations between side streets and main thoroughfare. They can see the disparities in positions occupied by people with evident access to power and capital and those who lack such access. They can gain some sense of the historical, geographical and cultural forces that have shaped the community. They have what within the educational field Bourdieu calls the 'scholastic point of view'.

Scholastic point of view

The scholastic point of view is the objectifying and universalising perspective offered by a position within the academy. This privileged position comes with a price. Not only does our spectator on the hill reflect on the structural relations and cultural forces that shape the town; they are also required to reflect upon the relations and forces that underlie their own position, and which therefore make it particular and situated.

In making this point, Bourdieu would challenge what he would regard as crude universalising perspectives that take the particular terms of reference of one field position and apply it to the world at large. For example, sociological concepts like that of 'underclass', which emerge from a particular intellectual and social milieu—the American sociological field—should not be taken as a universal precept and applied to another social context—say studies of class relations in Brazil—where such a term has no currency or relevance.

Bourdieu's practical vision for the academy is, through the mechanism of the scholastic point of view, to work towards universalising 'the conditions of access to universality' (1998d: 137). In the context of the moves towards making tertiary education a universal experience for people in the western world, Bourdieu is suggesting that the objectifying tendencies and reflexive practice his ideas promote will assist students in both reflecting on the structural relations that 'speak' through them, and intervening in a positive manner within the social world.

We need to qualify this position. After all, Bourdieu is also critical of the scholastic point of view because it is a view fashioned from the particular social conditions which prevail within the university, and its applicability to different social contexts is strictly limited. We can suggest, however, that the universalising tendencies generated through the scholastic point of view can assist in bringing about practical political action on the basis of two claims. First, to the extent that the scholastic point of view is self-reflexive, it is potentially empowering (at least intellectually and discursively) for those people who are exposed to it. Second, the academy's position as a dominated faction within a dominant class has the potential to help it empathise with the circumstances experienced by other dominated groups, while at the same time having access to literacies and positions of power that can assist these dominated groups. It should be pointed out, however, that this position is not without its problems and critics. John Frow, for instance, gives detailed and not unsympathetic consideration to the notion that 'the politics of intellectuals' can constitute 'a corporatism of the universal to the extent that it seeks to universalize the privileged conditions of their own existence', but finally dismisses it as a 'wrong argument' (Frow 1995: 168). Such a proposition 'relies for all its force on a distinction between "real" intellectuals and "pseudo"-intellectuals' (1995: 168), which effectively destroys the notion of an intellectual class faction (after all, who is authorised to identify the 'authentic' members of the class?). He also points to two other flaws in the argument. First, he argues, Bourdieu 'massively overestimates the social value of intellectual work' (1995: 168). And second, there is nothing to substantiate the claim that the interests of the intellectual class (even if it could be 'authenticated') coincide with those of other social classes. These issues will be dealt with again, in Chapter 10, when we discuss the relation between the field of cultural production, the field of journalism, and 'market forces'.

Practical and other reason

An important aspect of this project is Bourdieu's vision of the relationship between practical reason and the forms of reason promoted by the academy. Practical reason, as a dimension of habitus, is the capacity people have to make sense of, and negotiate, the situations they are confronted with in the social world: driving a car, choosing which dress to wear, calculating moves in a football game that will maximise the chance of scoring a goal. The academy, on the other hand, has tended to be regarded historically as a site for the promotion of a higher form of reason; the capacity to make rational judgements, which equips people to practise law, conduct scientific experiments, solve mathematical problems, theorise about historical conditions and so forth.

The German philosopher Immanuel Kant suggests this version of reason is a 'human faculty' (something which separates us from the beasts in the field) which educational institutions are equipped to promote. According to the traditional procedures of the academy, as students evolve through the learning process they become able to master progressively more elevated dimensions of this human faculty. For example, Bloom's taxonomy has become a standard educational tool for evaluating to what extent students have progressed up the scale of intellectual complexity from simple recall of facts through analysis to higher level skills such as synthesising and evaluating evidence. Similarly, the educational psychologist Jean Piaget's theory of human development has informed pedagogy in terms of calculating at what stage and age the student should be expected to progress to higher intellectual tasks.

We should recognise that conceiving of reason in this way as a human faculty subject to a hierarchy is a significant dimension of the academy's work of making distinctions and reproducing social divisions. It is assumed that only particularly gifted and cultivated individuals will have access to the higher faculties of reason, and therefore be able to access privileged positions within the academy and beyond it to the social world.

In challenging this belief, Bourdieu seeks to emphasise that 'reason', like other human faculties and values, is always connected as a sense-making mechanism to the position from which the social agent acts. Hence, working out a move to score a goal in football is just as much an act of reason as working through a philosophical proposition from Wittgenstein; they simply occur in different contexts and have their own demands.

Bourdieu to see with—metaliteracies

We can link Bourdieu's concepts of practical reason and the scholastic point of view with the idea of cultural literacy, as a way of seeing the world. In one study of Bourdieu's work, Richard Jenkins claimed that he was 'good to think with' (1992: 11). On the basis of this discussion of his contribution to the educational field, we can also argue that Bourdieu is also very good to see with.

We have seen throughout this chapter how positions within the educational field are distributed and performed according to a certain degree of blindness, or near-sightedness. As Bourdieu comments, the unconscious dimension of the habitus means that social agents tend not to reflect on the forces that dispose them to act and behave as they do. We have seen how a Cambridge Professor of English can be blind to the fact that his class largely consists of females; how the American academic field can be blind to other cultural contexts; how professors can be blind to the failure of their communication processes to reach students effectively. More generally, agents within the educational field tend to be blind to the objective structural relations and institutional processes that speak through them.

Bourdieu's studies and ideas can help us to see through this blindness. They help us to draw out those institutional processes and structural relations that lurk behind every action made within the educational field, from the clever turn of phrase uttered within a lecture to the dress sense, hairstyle and walking manner of a professor or student. In a sense, Bourdieu's ideas provide us with a set of literacies that enable us to 'read' various scenarios within the educational field and negotiate them effectively.

Thus when we read as feedback on an assignment a professor chastising students for crude expression or alternatively praising them for their sensitivity or elegance of exposition, we can see how these judgements are being shaped. In a sense the field is speaking through the professor and disposing her to make judgements on that student's capacity to fulfil the role of a cultivated personality. We can further see how the cultivation of a cultivated personality ties in with the university's role of reproducing distinction; that is, the way of acting that helps distinguish upper from lower classes and naturalises social inequalities.

In this situation a literate student will be able to give the university system what it wants: that is, (re)produce a style that can be recognised and valued as 'cultivated', while at the same time being able to move beyond this cultivated style so as to communicate effectively in other contexts within other fields and with other audiences. While the unreflexive student is simply able to negotiate positions within the field on its terms (and according to its rules and values), the reflexive student is better equipped to move across different positions on terms that are at least partially their own. Thus they have greater ownership of their cultural trajectory—that is, their movement across and between different field positions throughout their lives.

This is significant, because a university education is not dedicated simply to providing students in discipline-specific skills knowledge in a particular field, but in providing them, ideally, with sets of generic skills that provide them with a form of distinction over people who have not been university-educated. And this can translate into capital outside their immediate academic field: in 2000, for instance, an Australian survey found that what employers looked for in graduates, beyond the basic skills to do the job, were qualities like critical thinking, creativity, problem-solving skills and good oral communication. These findings tend to be typical of employer expectations throughout the western world. For example, a computer company in the United States was reputedly more inclined to employ graduates with a literary studies background than a computer programming degree because they valued the literature majors' ability to think imaginatively.

Bourdieu's ideas pick up on these valued qualities but give them a particular focus. For him, values like creativity and the ability to think critically, like the 'human faculty' of reason discussed earlier, are not situated 'out there' as some kind of higher intellectual faculty to which we all might aspire but only the truly gifted among us will ever really reach. Rather, these values are always situated within a particular context and have to do with the way of negotiating the position in which they are encountered. They have less to do with mastering a particular taxonomy or progressing through various stages of intellectual development; and more to do with the reflexive practice that helps secure one a feel for the game as it confronts one through a particular site.

Yet, particularised as Bourdieu's view of human faculties is, these faculties are also mobile in the sense that they equip one to consider the different perspectives and positions that constitute the social world. We can return to our image of the person looking upon the town from the privileged position of a hill. Beyond reflecting on their own grounds for seeing the town as they do, they might also draw upon Bourdieu's theoretical principles to consider how this community may appear to other people, based on their various positions within it. They might then reflect upon the way they too can appear (that is, communicate) differently to differently situated individuals in order to bring about practical effects.

We could refer to this capacity to move across different perspectives and affect ways of seeing and appearing as 'metaliteracy' (Schirato & Yell 2000). If literacy involves the capacity to read the situation and game from a particular perspective, metaliteracy involves the capacity to move strategically into different positions in one's reading of the situation and the game. An example would be a group of students studying the field of multimedia. Some might be particularly literate in the techniques of multimedia, able to manipulate the various computer-generated images to create aesthetically pleasing and engaging web sites and so forth. Others might be less literate in the techniques, but particularly skilled in understanding how the images can be marketed. In each case, the students have *literacies*; but they will only develop *metaliteracy* to the extent that they are able to understand each other's areas of knowledge, and respond to the different perspectives other people may bring to multimedia. For example, someone from a different cultural background may feel alienated by the technology and want to have nothing to do with multimedia. A bank, on the other hand, may be very sceptical about the financial soundness of young people working in such an enterprise and be reluctant to lend them the money to boost their career. Others again may feel that multimedia, as an emergent technology, could be open to abuse and have a morally corrupting influence on its practitioners. Each student will be faced with developing different strategies for engaging with these perspectives in order to boost their access to capital and socially consecrated positions.

Conclusion

In this chapter we have looked at the implications of Bourdieu's work for the study of higher education. We have seen how:

- Bourdieu identifies a range of techniques through which institutions of higher education are able to secure the distinction between teacher and students, and between the world of the academy and the social world beyond;
- different disciplines within the field have varying degrees of access to social authority and to different forms of capital;
- the scholastic point of view offers students a particularised but universalising perspective on the world at large; and
- students can follow Bourdieu's idea to help them develop metaliteracies that will help them negotiate different positions and perspectives within the social world.

We might return to the issue we raised at the beginning of Chapter 6: to what extent can education be a force for social transformation, and to what extent is it an instrument of social reproduction? Through Bourdieu's conceptual apparatus, he is able to identify how education acts to promote social distinction and, as such, operate as an agent of reproduction of the cultural arbitrary. But he does not see it as merely a site of reproduction of the status quo. 'Science', he writes, quoting Auguste Comte, 'leads to foresight, and foresight leads to action' (1998c: 55). So Bourdieu also sees education as potentially transformative, particularly in the fact that a focus on reflexive practice and the development of metaliteracies can help give students a stake in the game played within the field of education, and some measure of control over its outcomes. In other words, within its reproductive tendencies, the education system can be manipulated to bring about certain transformations.

In the next chapters we consider the implications of Bourdieu's ideas for the fields of cultural production and, more specifically, art.

Further reading

Bourdieu, Pierre 1998d, *Practical Reason: On the Theory of Action*, Polity Press, Cambridge, Ch 6.
Schirato, Tony and Susan Yell 2000, *Communication and Cultural Literacy*, 2nd edn, Allen & Unwin/Sage, Sydney and London

8

The field of cultural production

Bourdieu was a photographer, so it is perhaps not surprising that, after looking at institutionalised social practices like marriage and education, he should turn his attention to creative practices. His interest in what he calls 'the field of cultural production' was evident in some of his earliest publications. The original French language publication of *Photography: A Middle-brow Art*, his study of the social functions of photography, was published in 1965; in 1967 his translation of German art historian Erwin Panofsky's *Gothic Architecture and Scholastic Thought* (with an introduction written by Bourdieu) was published, and in 1969 Bourdieu published the findings of his research into the uses of art museums (*The Love of Art*).

Bourdieu's approach to the field of cultural production is similar to Panofsky's, because neither is interested in simply observing aesthetic trends or tendencies. Rather, what both scholars do is analyse the relationship between ways of understanding the world, and the sort of creative works that are made in a particular place and time. In fact, Bourdieu's main concern is not with aesthetics—which is, at its simplest, the question of beauty—but with the principles behind people's tastes: why do some people spend their time and energy in making cultural products? Why do some people buy (for instance) paintings or theatre tickets? How does it help them to organise their world? What meanings are attached to these sorts of practices? The reason for his interest in these questions is that:

> There is no way out of the game of culture; and one's only
> chance of objectifying the true nature of the game is to
> objectify as fully as possible the very operations which one is
> obliged to use in order to achieve that objectification.
> (1984: 12)

If there really is 'no way out of the game', our best option is to
understand the game, and work out the most appropriate and
useful ways of playing it. Bourdieu's writings on the field of
cultural production go some distance to help us understand the
'game', and play it more effectively. His findings are published
in a number of articles, and in several of his books: *Distinction*
(1984) is perhaps the most important and certainly the best known
of all these writings, and here he explores the relation between
artistic taste and social background; *The Love of Art* (1991e) is the
publication of a major study in which Bourdieu and his team
surveyed over nine thousand art museum visitors across France;
Photography is an analysis of how French people used and valued
photography during the period of his research; and both
The Field of Cultural Production (1993c) and *The Rules of Art* (1996b)
develop the ideas he opens up in the earlier books, and also
provide a historical and literary analysis of the (primarily
nineteenth-century) artist's identity. Finally, in *Free Exchange*
(1995), an extended 'conversation' between himself and the New
York-based visual artist Hans Haacke, he explores contemporary
art practice and the creative habitus.

The consistent feature in all these writings is the attention
Bourdieu pays to the effect of social and political structures on
aesthetic taste, and on what he calls 'practices of distinction'. But,
convincing as his arguments and research data are, his position
at times becomes somewhat essentialising, as John Frow points
out in his critique of Bourdieu's work on the field of cultural
production, *Cultural Studies and Cultural Value* (1995). Frow argues
that Bourdieu tends to collapse various social groups and various
social experiences into a single group, a single experience, in the
interests of arguing for a dominant field-specific logic. For
instance, in positing a group of people who share an 'aesthetic
disposition' and its related experiences, Bourdieu describes
people from a number of very different social backgrounds as

though they belonged to a single 'class'. And similarly, he tends to treat all aesthetic experiences as though they had a single underpinning logic. But in fact, of course, the adolescent rock guitarist, the 'cultivated' lover of opera, and the avant garde writer are likely to have very little in common with one another in terms of either social origins or aesthetic tastes, beyond their shared membership of the field of cultural production—a field with a multitude of positions, practices, logics and values.

An effect of this reductive view, Frow points out, is 'a binary construction of the concepts of a "high" and "popular" aesthetic understood as something like class languages, fixed and ahistorical class dispositions with a necessary categorical structure' (1995: 31). In other words, Bourdieu tends to reproduce the dominant discourses of the field of cultural production, correlating artistic tastes and interests with functionlessness, with disinterest, and with the upper classes; and 'popular' tastes and interests with functionality, with social or economic interest, and with the working classes. This is a curious blindness in Bourdieu's writings, since in other texts (and even in sections of his 'cultural field' texts) he argues against such an approach. But, as Frow again suggests, Bourdieu's surprising lack of reflexivity when it comes to the field of cultural production may well stem from the fact that he sees the aesthetic realm as, primarily, the site for the exercise of social dominance, and 'forgets' the other issues involved. That is, Bourdieu's notion is that 'culture' is the domain of those who, by virtue of their class, status and education, are possessed of 'cultivated' tastes, and able, by virtue of the same sorts of capital, to inscribe these tastes as being at the same time natural, and the markers of a natural superiority.

We can partially agree with him here. Certainly, those who possess knowledge at least of 'high art' codes do in fact tend to be better educated, and often 'upper class', as he showed so convincingly in *Distinction*. However, Bourdieu does not provide convincing evidence that the importance of the aesthetic realm extends beyond this group. There is little to indicate that people outside this group have any real interest in—or, more importantly, any real reverence for—the field, and its discourses and practices.

In fact, the 'truths' of the aesthetic so dearly held by Bourdieu's 'cultivated classes' may be no more than a kind of illusio—a 'truth' believed only by those who already have an investment in the 'game of culture', and disregarded by those outside the field. As Frow writes, 'it may well be the case, particularly since the massive growth of a television culture in which working-class people tend to be fully competent, that high culture, or rather the *prestige* of high culture, has become largely irrelevant to them' (Frow, 1995: 37).

In these final three chapters we engage with Bourdieu's writings on the field of cultural production. In this chapter, we describe the general principles and structure of the field. Then, bearing in mind the strained relations between the aesthetic ('art for art's sake') pole and the socially and economically responsive pole of the field of cultural production, we will discuss them independently: in Chapter 9 we look at what Bourdieu terms 'the restricted sub-field' of artistic production (specifically, the generally autonomous pole of the field); and in Chapter 10 we deal with his more recent writings on what he calls the sub-field of 'large-scale production'—popular culture and the media (that is, the more heteronomous pole of the field). But in order to 'map' the field, we will first define what is generally meant by the term 'art', and thus distinguish it from general culture and popular culture.

What is art?

As virtually any textbook on art will testify, the term refers to practices and institutions connected with creative production. These include plastic and visual arts and crafts, writing, music and the performance arts—all those objects and practices which, Panofsky writes, 'demand to be experienced aesthetically' (1955: 11). While they may also have a function (jazz music doubles as a mode of entertainment, a ceramic jar may also be used for storage), the goods and services produced in this field are not made so that they will be functional; they are intended to be, first of all, *aesthetic*. In other words, the things produced in the field of cultural production are in the first instance symbolic rather

149

than material. They are primarily designed not to make money, but to make some sort of statement about the artist's vision or the social universe. Hence, the argument goes, they are made under the principle of 'disinterestedness'.

One of the most significant things about Bourdieu's work on the field of cultural production is that it breaks with this romantic idea—still associated with art, despite all the evidence to the contrary—that creative production is a sort of 'social magic', or a 'special language of grace' (or charisma). This implies that the creative world is somehow divorced from the everyday world and its demands, and that creative practitioners—and their audiences, 'people of distinction'—are specially gifted, specially sensitive, and specially alert beings. By analysing this world, he is able to show that in fact it is organised, regulated and structured like other social fields: its rules, discourses, narratives, agents, institutions, specific capital and so on can all be identified. And in identifying these, Bourdieu takes pains to demystify cultural practice, and show that it comes out of a set of social conditions, and performs a set of social functions.

All the same, the principle of disinterest is a dominant theme in its discourses. That is, art and artists, as the site and subjects of charisma (a special gift), do not need economic or social approval: they work 'for art's sake' alone. This makes the field of cultural production an important site for crafting meanings, social forms and social relations, and finding ways to make sense of them. If the field is in fact 'disinterested', it can be presented as something that tells the truth because it has no investment—no 'interest'—in pleasing the government or sponsors, or in attracting buyers. And because this field is dedicated to making meanings—that is, to its symbolic function—cultural products can be seen as indicators of how members of a society perceive themselves and their values. Those bodies of work that become well known and important—that come to be 'named' as, say, British art, or American dance—are also indicators of the authorised vision of that society, and particularly of how the dominant institutions see their society and want it to be seen by others. Because of this, according to Bourdieu, the field of cultural production has symbolic power, and its products are among the means by which a society—including its way of life and its sets of values—is objectified.

This symbolic function is associated with another important discourse of this field, which suggests that culture makes the invisible visible, and brings into material form the unexpressed conditions of being. The 1990s grunge music style, for instance, with its harsh guitar riffs and anguished lyrics, made visible the angst of being young in a society that is often hostile to youth, and provided a 'voice' and a sense of identity for some young people. Norwegian painter Edvard Munch, with his haunting (and haunted) painting *The Scream* (1893), rendered a sense of existential fear in a disturbed, disturbing atmosphere that, in the first decades of the twentieth century in Europe, expressed for many people the dread and anguish of that period.

Because creative work is able to make the invisible visible, and produce symbolic representations, associations are often drawn between art and religion or magic. The Frankfurt School writer Theodor Adorno, and the sociologists of art, Arnold Foster and Judith Blau (among others), say that art performs a 'social magic'; while Bourdieu writes that art is 'the sacred sphere of culture' (1984: 7), and a 'religion' dedicated to 'the question of cultural salvation in the language of grace' (1991e: 1). Certainly the fields of art, religion and magic all conjure up particular kinds of 'reality', all depend on a combination of imagination and belief, and all are committed to a certain mysticism. With religion, there is the idea that a supreme being exists and can be contacted. With magic, there is the notion that forms can change through the application of the language of power. And for culture, there is a belief in the sleight of hand which turns an ordinary 'thing' into an 'Artwork'.

But people have not always treated the field of cultural production with a reverent attitude. In the European Middle Ages, for instance, the word 'art' did not mean what it does now—the product or process that has aesthetics as its primary identity. Rather, 'art' just meant skill—any skill, be it conversation, carpentry or collage. It was not until about the eighteenth century that people began to regard art as a 'calling' invested with 'grace' or 'faith', something capable of representing and transforming the social world.

Distinction

But this does not explain what art is; a point Bourdieu is quick to make (and to answer). For Bourdieu, 'culture' (the whole social world) and 'Culture' (art) exist in a close relationship, because something can only be identified as art if it is found in a context (say, an art museum) that is recognised as artistic; and/or if it is made by someone who is known to be an artist; and/or if those authorised to make such judgments tell us that in fact it is art. In other words, something becomes art only when it is named as such by figures of legitimation—or gatekeepers (important curators, publishers, established artists, critics and reviewers, and so on).

Still, there really is not any general agreement about what or who should be included as part of the field of cultural production. A walk around an art museum—particularly one showing an exhibition of contemporary work—is bound to give you the opportunity to hear someone complain that something 'isn't art', or that 'my 5-year-old could have made that'. And even within the creative world there is often heated disagreement about whether someone is an 'artist' or merely a 'tradesperson', or a 'wordsmith'. What this points out is that art is not magical or immanent: it does not exist evidentially in and of itself. Rather, it is a social artefact, the product of a field, and it comes into existence through a process of field-specific competition. This, like any competition in any field, comes down to a question of power—who is authorised to speak for, or attribute value to, various positions in the field?

The 'prize' in this competition is becoming recognised as a regulator of the field (that is, a gatekeeper) and, in addition, there is the chance to accrue the true reward for success in the field of cultural production—symbolic capital, which Bourdieu describes as *capital* 'misrecognized as capital' (1990b: 118). That is to say, it is 'capital' because, like money or status, it legitimates differences in social class and social importance. It is misrecognised as such because it is not recognised as a form of capital. Instead, we tend to see it as being someone's natural or inherent quality, rather than something that a person has acquired through competition, inherited from their family, or learned in school. In both *The Love of*

Art and *Distinction*, for instance, Bourdieu shows that the ability to appreciate art, and possession of a taste for art, are closely connected to one's education and 'class' status. Middle-class people in these studies were far more confident than working-class people about approaching cultural products and cultural institutions. Bourdieu's argument was that this was because they had acquired conceptual skills and social confidence from their families and their middle-class schools, rather than because they were born mysteriously possessed of a 'natural' love of art. In other words, their social origins and training provided them with symbolic capital, which Bourdieu also describes as *consecration, distinction* or *prestige.*

The idea that a taste for art is learned rather than inherent is not (or was not in 1969, when *The Love of Art* was first published) something that is generally recognised. Art museums are public property, the story goes, and open to everyone in society. If working-class people do not visit such museums, they must be excluding themselves. And this is further read as 'proof' that working-class people inevitably lack 'taste'—oddly associated almost exclusively with middle-class people—for art.

Bourdieu, of course, takes issue with this. The main message of both *The Love of Art* and *Distinction* is that the design and structure of cultural institutions tend to exclude people who do not have the appropriate background or capital, and that they perform this exclusion while giving the appearance of being available to everyone. Working-class people tend not to go to such places, Bourdieu suggests, because they are not sure how to behave, and the institutions do not make themselves 'user-friendly'.

This is no longer necessarily the case, of course; many state art and heritage museums have access and education programs, clear wall texts and easily available didactic material, all designed to make themselves more widely accessible. All the same, what counts as 'good taste' is still largely decided by institutions and individuals who are not necessarily inclined to be user-friendly, because taste depends on what Bourdieu calls the 'cultural arbitrary'. This is his way of describing the effect whereby things (whether practices, products, or values) are made to seem universally significant because they are important to dominant people and institutions, and because they come to be inscribed in the habitus and supported by the values and discourses of the general social field. Bourdieu gives wonderful examples of the cultural arbitrary in *Outline*, where he describes the patterns of life and behaviour of the Kabyle people in Algeria. Women and men, he writes, have their own particular way of walking—a man has a 'steady and determined pace', a woman 'is expected to walk with a slight stoop' (1977a: 94)—and this is not for any obvious reason except to reinforce the system of values that 'proves' that men are 'manly' and assured, and women are modest and restrained. And this is the purely arbitrary effect of a set of cultural principles and systems of evaluation, which come to seem natural through the workings of the habitus. Bourdieu writes, 'As an acquired [and arbitrary] system of generative schemes objectively adjusted to the particular conditions in which it is constituted, the habitus engenders all the thoughts, all the perceptions, and all the actions consistent with those conditions, and no others' (1977a: 95).

Art is, Bourdieu insists, part of the field of power (1984: 7), so when it comes to the field of cultural production, the 'cultural arbitrary' ensures that the things that are valued by dominant people, institutions (public schools, state theatres) and events (the Booker Prize for literature, the Cannes Film Festival) are valued (at least in principle) by everyone—whether they actually like them, or use them, or not. As an example, a major research project carried out in Australia by the government's arts funding body found that a significant number of people surveyed said that they were proud of, and consider that Australia benefits from, Australian art, though 80 per cent of them recorded that they do not actually engage with art—they neither make nor use high culture products. And what this means is that authorised art has a social rather than a personal function. 'I don't know much about art, but I know what I like' does not simply describe someone's aesthetic judgement, but more precisely establishes their educational and class background—and establishes it, at least within dominant circles, as less valuable than that of someone who does 'know about art'.

Culture and power

The point that Bourdieu takes from this is that aesthetic judgements are not made on the basis of an abstract or universal standard. Rather, something becomes 'culture' because it is in someone's (or some institution's) interests for this to be so. And the 'someones' able to promote their personal interest include the government, the education system, major cultural institutions, and important gatekeepers—or, in Bourdieu-speak, the dominant. It is for this reason that sociologists and cultural theorists find the field of cultural production particularly interesting. Art, as we noted earlier, is not simply 'aesthetic'; it is a symbolic thing, and symbols, Bourdieu writes, 'make it possible for there to be a *consensus* on the meaning of the social world, a consensus which contributes fundamentally to the reproduction of the social order' (1991a: 166).

What Bourdieu is suggesting here is that symbols (creative products especially, in this context) actually construct society by providing things and people with a specifically *social* being, by contributing to their being publicly recognised. Think, for instance, of 1950s British 'angry young man' theatre, exemplified by John Osborne's play *Look Back in Anger* (1956). Now, the angry young man was not a new type of person who emerged suddenly in the 1950s—there are quite ancient writings that complain about 'young people' and their attitudes—but what the field of cultural production did was bring them to the attention of the public, to represent them as a group-in-itself. Rap music has done much the same thing for urban disenfranchised young African-American men in the 1990s, while television programs like *Friends* or *Suddenly Susan*, and movies like *Threesome* or *Swingers*, have similarly made 'twenty-somethings' visible as a self-aware community, recognised by the wider society.

So creative works do not just render visible the aesthetic world or the imaginings of a group of gifted people; they also provide a site in which general social relations can be represented and negotiated. Because of this, it is not only aesthetic and symbolic, but also *political*—not distanced from, or disinterested in, the everyday world, but deeply embedded in relations of

155

power. As Bourdieu puts it, 'Culture is unifying' (1994a: 7).

We saw above that in *Distinction* and *The Love of Art* Bourdieu suggests that the field of cultural production is divisive because it contributes to social distinctions. Why, then, would he also say that culture is unifying? This is because although its products do, of course, divide us into those with taste and those without, they also produce symbols of 'us'—the national community. This means the field of cultural production can fulfil the function of social integration, by structuring what Bourdieu calls the 'principles of vision and division' of the social world. This is most obvious in cultural products authorised by totalitarian regimes. Think, for instance, òf Socialist Realist art, the style established by the Soviet state in the 1930s as the official standard for creative work. Socialist Realism was designed to glorify the political and social ideals of communism, and was heroic in scope and scale, dedicated to idealising and validating the Soviet state, its leaders and its people. The principles of vision and division it represented were that the world was divided into 'us' (Soviets) and 'them' (capitalists etc.); and that 'Soviet' equalled healthy, strong, noble, honest and so on. All modern nations lay claim to a body of art that represents them; but in non-totalitarian states their involvement is usually less obvious— disguised in the form of cultural grants and awards, for instance, rather than being enshrined in policy.

Culture and the government

This brings us to the relationship between the field of cultural production and the government. We made the point that this field is one of the sites in which identity is developed, because members of a community organise themselves into social groups partly on the basis of taste (opera goers versus football fans, for instance), or because a cultural product or form gives them a visible social identity ('twenty-somethings' being represented as a specific community in popular television). We also discussed 'culture's' role as a site for the exercise of symbolic power: something that makes it attractive to governments, and means that it can be used to provide indicators of nationhood. In fact, it seems to be practically mandatory for a state to possess national art if it is to be able to claim to be a distinct nation. The UNESCO convention on cultural property protection (1970) notes that: 'cultural property constitutes one of the basic elements of civilization and national culture'. Major state institutions tend to support this point of view: state museums, for instance, usually organise their collections according to national as well as temporal origins (a gallery of contemporary Japanese art or artefacts will be separated from traditional European art or artefacts); or a university literature course might offer subjects titled 'The nineteenth-century French novel', 'English theatre', or 'The American short story'.

While the idea of a 'national culture' may be pervasive, it is not easy to pin it down. For instance, the term 'British art' seems to be describing a homogeneous 'Britain'; but as we discuss in Chapter 5, Britain does not have an inherent and unproblematic existence. It really only exists in so far as it is produced by authorised discourses, practices and institutions, such as the *British* Broadcasting Commission, or the *British* Arts Council. Nor does the term 'British art' actually mean anything coherent or consistent: what relationship, for instance, do Damien Hirst and his dead cows have to Blandford Fletcher and his nineteenth-century social realist paintings? Like any other national entity, 'Britain' is a fabricated melange of communities of interest who may have little or nothing in common with one another, except for the fact that they are all regulated by something called 'the British government'. Still, these fragments of 'the nation' can be welded together, at least momentarily, by the representations of 'us' that we see in story or performance or visual form. And this is why governments take an interest in the field of cultural production. By managing that field, the state can manage how we think about our social world and its organisation.

Bourdieu does not suggest that the field of cultural production meekly obeys governmental dictates. Instead, he shows that the dominant discourse of disinterestedness means that art always leans to independence rather than being enmeshed in state interest. In fact, art is used as often to criticise government as to support it. But creative practitioners do face a dilemma: for art that is avant garde, or done purely 'for art's sake', there really is not a market in which it can be sold. Artists, of course, still have to eat and pay rent, and if they cannot make a direct living from their art, they will apply for government grants and other support. And this support comes with strings attached, because cultural policy—which organises how the state's budget will be distributed—regulates what counts as (authorised) culture, and who is authorised to produce it. By doing this, the state arts board can take ownership of art and can put it to its own uses. And one 'use' that appears consistently in cultural policies, as Jonathan Pick pointed out in his 1988 study of the British arts funding system, is the constitution of a unified community.

This point—that this apparently disinterested and heterogeneous field in fact has both structure and function—is one that Bourdieu returns to throughout his writings on creative practice. The field is, he writes, a *'structured* structure' because its products (artworks and their meanings or 'visions') are communicated through the structures of the field. In the case of a movie, for instance, the structures would include the studio system through which it was made, the distribution network, the censorship boards, the advertising and review systems and so on. But it is also what he calls a *'structuring* structure' because it provides the means for understanding 'the world'. So 'culture' is not just the product of a particular social organisation; it also shapes society by the representations it makes, and by how it chooses to make those representations.

Think, for instance, of the 1999 movie *Fight Club*. Through the structure of the movie medium and its various institutions, we are introduced to the unnamed character played by Edward Norton. We participate vicariously in his life, watching the events that befall him, empathising with him, becoming familiar with the way he negotiates his job, his physical condition and his friendships. But the movie also has a structuring dimension, because it makes representations about the public sphere. In various story lines which deal with identity, the symbolic order, legal and economic institutions, and alienation, the movie explores and makes visible what it means to be male, especially working-class

male, in the technologised late twentieth century. And consequently, Norton's character becomes for his audiences not just
what he calls a 'single serve friend', but what Bourdieu calls a
'symbol of a social position' (1996b: 5). He represents, and in this
way contributes to, the structure, the relationships and the designs
of the social world.

Art is a mechanism that makes our imaginings 'real' and, in
making visible the beliefs and cultural codes that are shared by
a community, generates the social matrix. This locates it within
the field of power, which explains the close relationship it has
with the government, for instance. But as a field, it is not particularly powerful itself. In fact, Bourdieu places it at the dominated
end of the field of power. This is for several reasons. First, as we
noted earlier, artistic discourses insist that art should be done 'for
art's sake', not for economic profit. In fact, art that is produced
principally for financial return is considered 'not art', or at any
rate inferior. Second, according to its discourse of disinterestedness, art is not supposed to be directly engaged in sociopolitical
action. Although some artists have a very overt political practice,
most say that they are making art for its own sake. It may, they
agree, have a political effect, but its reason for being is aesthetic.

The structure of the field

This is not the only story told about art, of course. Like
any field, the field of cultural production has a number of competing discourses and values. Bourdieu describes the field as
bifurcated, divided by two sets of values, practices and principles of production which he calls the 'autonomous' and the
'heteronomous' poles. At the 'heteronomous' pole artistic production is treated much like any other form of production: the work
is made work for a pre-established market, with the aim of achieving commercial success. Here we find things like airport novels,
advertising jingles, school holiday movies and the sort of water-
colour paintings you can buy at a tourist market. Producers at
this end of the field are not as concerned with looking within
themselves or to one another for inspiration; rather, they obey

pre-existing demands for particular types of work, and use pre-established forms.

Because of the field's rules about what counts as art, work done under the heteronomous principle of production is often coded as being not 'real' art. But works produced under this logic are still art (because they are part of the field), and can maintain their claims to a position within the field by 'avoiding the crudest forms of mercantilism and by abstaining from fully revealing their self-interested goals' (1996b: 142). Heteronomous artists will often insist that they are, after all, *artists*, often by adding the word 'art' or 'artist' in their job title. Think of advertising executives, for instance, who are often called 'art directors' or a similar term. The point in doing this is that unless people working at this end of the field can stake a claim to the field of cultural production, they cannot acquire any of the symbolic capital attached to art; in fact, they might as well spend their time designing washing machines, rather than competing for the consecration that comes with being an artist.

This consecration belongs most obviously at the 'autonomous' pole of the field, the site of 'art for arts sake'. Here, in what Bourdieu calls a 'reversal of economic logic', economic success is considered artistic failure—and vice versa. Bourdieu deals extensively with this principle in *Field*, and points out how clearly it demonstrates that reward need not be financial. In fact, artists may well serve their own interests by rejecting economic rewards or other commercial markers of success. The Academy Awards (Oscars) are an example of this; while they indicate success in industry terms, they also tend to indicate artistic failure (the thirteen Oscars won by the mammoth film *Titanic* are often used, in 'art film' circles, as proof that artistic death equals studio triumph).

The principles of production at the autonomous pole include imagination, truth and freedom from social or economic influence. Unlike heteronomous art, which relies on everyday literacies, and targets the general public as their audience, the expected audiences for work produced under this set of values is the *cognoscenti*—other artists, art critics, those who have acquired the specialised education that will allow them to understand the 'in'-jokes, the intertextual references and the self-referentiality of the works. And the rewards in this part of the field are symbolic capital. Of course, symbolic capital can easily be transformed into economic capital, because once an artwork is recognised as 'excellent', people will be more inclined to purchase it or reproductions of it, to pay royalties or buy theatre tickets to view it. But while producers at the autonomous end of the field may indeed make money in this way, they would argue that this is not what drives their production—they are captives of the 'art for art's sake' rule.

Economic relations

The autonomous part of the field is not unified, however; it is divided between what Bourdieu calls the 'avant garde' and the 'consecrated'. We will discuss this in more detail in the next chapter, and simply make the point here that there is an anomaly in the field's discourse. If the failure to accumulate economic capital or rejection of commercial success are markers of the possession of high levels of symbolic capital, then the true avant gardes—undiscovered geniuses like the grunge guitarists who jam in their garage but never try to score a gig, the poet who reads his work only in smoky cafes, or the maker of short films who shows her work only to other undiscovered film makers—should be more valuable than the consecrated—established artists like the South African novelist, J.M. Coetzee, or the British painter, Lucien Freud, who make much or all of their living from their art. But this is not the case; the consecrated artists are the more powerful agents in the field, and they not only attract the most symbolic capital—they frequently attract economic capital too.

This anomaly can be explained by the fact that, despite what is said about the field of cultural production, no artist or artwork occupies a pure position; they are always situated somewhere on a continuum between the two poles. If we look at the publishing sector, we can roughly map out this continuum, with the pulp romance publisher Mills & Boon, say, at the heteronomous end (since they publish in a pre-established form, for a pre-determined market, and with little or no obvious commitment to 'literary values'); Spinifex Press in Australia, arguably, straddling the consecrated and unconsecrated poles of the field (since it publishes what could be classified as exploratory literature, but for a pre-established market—women's interests); and Pan Picador (in Britain) or Alfred A. Knopf (in the United States) close to the autonomous end (since they take a more consciously consecrated position, publishing 'capital L' Literature in what are often exploratory forms).

So, even when art claims to be fully autonomous, the most 'disinterested' of practitioners are in fact likely to be applying some sort of economic calculation to their work. And they really have no choice if art is to have a social identity, and if they are going to be able to make a living. After all, as Bourdieu points out in *Rules*, if artists were truly free of social, political and economic influences, they would have no customers except each other. This means that to achieve success in the field (whether that success is measured by economic or symbolic returns), artists must find a balance between understanding and obeying the rules of art (such as valuing disinterestedness), and making concessions to the economic field (a certain 'practical turn' which takes into account protecting one's economic rights, and accounting for the financial cost of production and distribution). And even the most elevated and consecrated artists have often been assiduous in this—there are numerous stories about how Picasso insisted on protecting the economic, as well as the artistic, value of his work; and Beethoven, Bourdieu records, was famous for defending his economic interests (in particular, those related to copyright on his scores).

Still, Bourdieu suggests that there are problems with seeing art as an economic product or process, because it is not easy to apply a direct commodity value to artistic products. First, many arts products are freely available in the public domain—for example, as free-to-air radio or television programs, in free-entry museums and public libraries, or as public (outdoor) art such as civic sculpture. And if they are available to 'us all', they are part of what economists call 'the commons'—no one can have exclusive possession of the objects, so they cannot be treated like any other commodity, or have a economically-calculated price attached to them. So, while at some level art objects are commodities, they are not usually *destined* to be commoditised.

Second, art works are not like other commodities because they rarely have an obvious use or function, and so again they do not easily or logically attract an economic value. Because of this, Bourdieu writes, 'Cultural production . . . must produce not only the object in its materiality, but also the value of this object' (1993c: 164). Again we can see the impossibility of 'really' dividing artistic production between the autonomous and heteronomous poles. Virtually all art work is simultaneously both autonomous and heteronomous. Art 'for art's sake' must still be marketed, if only to other agents in the art world, because unless it can be seen, nobody will know it has been made, and effectively it will not exist. Art made for a pre-existing market is still capital-A Art, because it typically attracts its dollar value not just because it has a particular function which can be directly evaluated financially (the cost of its individual components and labour hours, for example), but because of its association with the (consecrated) field of arts. Perhaps the most famous example of this effect is Marcel Duchamp's work *Fountain* (1917). This is, of course, no more than a commonplace urinal, but because Duchamp mounted it like a sculpture and placed it in an art exhibition as a legitimate piece of work; and because Duchamp was already a significant artist; and because the urinal was separated from its status as an object of utility and associated instead with other art objects, it became Art, and came to be seen as valuable both aesthetically and economically.

While objects may have another function or another identity as commodities, when they move into the world of Culture their economic value is applied differently from objects in the mainstream commodity world. They circulate under a different order of logic and exchange from that of 'everyday' goods, because they are now used principally as signs of distinction, social division and privilege.

Conclusion

The field of cultural production is, Bourdieu shows, unifying, because the stories it tells in its various products and media provide a story of 'us', and represent us to ourselves and others. But it is also divisive; as Bourdieu states:

> the culture which unifies (the medium of communication) is also the culture which separates (the instrument of distinction) and which legitimates distinctions by forcing all other cultures (designated as sub-cultures) to define themselves by their distance from the dominant culture. (1991a: 167)

The field of cultural production makes concrete the difference between nations (China/Chinese art versus New Zealand/New Zealand art); and makes concrete the difference between members of the same nation (the *cognoscenti*—those who 'get' the David Lynch film *Eraserhead*, or value modern art—and the *barbarians*—those who think *Eraserhead* is dead boring, or who cannot see the point of a white room filled with white canvases). And it is symbolically powerful because these distinctions between nations, communities and individuals on the basis of taste and understanding appear to be natural and inherent, but in fact are the effects of the social order (stemming from differentiation in levels of income, education and consecration) and contribute to the maintenance of that order. So, while the field of cultural production is often presented as something transcendent, and distanced from everyday interests and necessities, in fact it is deeply invested in the social, political and economic fields. In the next chapter we will look in more detail at how individual art practitioners negotiate these fields.

In this chapter we have discussed Bourdieu's central findings on the field of cultural production:

- its bifurcated nature: divided between the autonomous principle of production (art for art's sake) and the heteronomous principle of production (works produced for a market);
- its position as the dominated area of the dominant part of society, because although it is associated with dominant (educated, 'upper class') sectors of the community, it has attentuated links with the economic field, and little direct political interest;

- its role in shaping community and national identity, because it produces images and stories that represent 'us' to ourselves and to others, and contributes to the reproduction of the social order;
- and while, as John Frow shows, Bourdieu has a tendency to universalise the importance of the field of cultural production, his work more generally is valuable in making sense of its principles and practices.

Further reading

Bourdieu, Pierre with Luc Boltanksi, Robert Castel, Jean-Claude Chamboredon, and Dominique Schnapper, 1990c, *Photography: A Middle-brow Art*, trans. Shaun Whiteside, Stanford University Press, Stanford, 'Introduction'

Foster, Arnold W. and Judith R. Blau (eds) 1989, *Art and Society: Readings in the Sociology of the Arts*, State University of New York Press, Albany

Jenkins, Richard 1992, *Pierre Bourdieu*, Routledge, London and New York, Ch 6

Robbins, Derek 1991, *The Work of Pierre Bourdieu: Recognizing Society*, Open University Press, Milton Keynes, Ch 8

9

Art and artists

In the previous chapter we discussed some of the broad brush-stroke issues Bourdieu develops when thinking about creative practice. Particularly, we looked at how he describes the main principles that structure the field of cultural production, and the relationship of that field to the social, economic and political fields. In this chapter we will take a more 'micro' approach, and discuss the place of individual creative agents: why they enter the field, and how the notions of habitus, capital and social class can be used to make sense of artistic practice.

What is an artist?

Art could not exist as a field unless there were people willing to produce artworks, to staff or otherwise service cultural institutions, and to promote and believe the discourses. But what it means to be an artist, and how the identity of 'artist' can be defined, has changed over the centuries. During the late nineteenth century and most of the twentieth century, for instance, artists were typically understood to be unique individuals, dedicated to their 'vocation', and imbued with a special charisma. This view of artists comes to us directly from the Romantic period in England and Europe, which placed enormous importance on imagination and beauty. But this is by no means the only perspective on how artists can be defined and understood. During the Middle Ages, as we noted in Chapter 8, artists were simply seen as skilled workers who plied their trade within collectives or guilds. By the Renaissance a change was becoming evident. Along with the rise of scientific investigation and the establishment of universities as places of specialised learning, artists were beginning to separate themselves from other workers, and from being seen as 'ordinary' practitioners in the general economy.

The charismatic, romantic (and Romantic) notion of the artist as independent, solitary and disinterested cannot, of course, be sustained. First, as a result of economic structures in the late twentieth century, artists in western countries have been brought back to something like the position they had before the Renaissance, again being dependent on patronage (in the form of arts grants and public art funding), which means they are also coming under a sort of hidden censorship—those who do not please the state are less likely to be funded. And second, if we look at what people in the field actually do, we find that artists are not really distanced from the social and economic world because they are dependent on a range of collective structures, processes, agents and institutions from the moment they conceive of an idea to when the finished artwork is let loose on a waiting world. Without suppliers of pigment, canvas and framing material, for instance, a painting could not be made; without curators, designers, gallery directors and art critics the painting would not be shown or discussed. The same thing applies to the other art forms, with practitioners dependent throughout the process of production on agents, editors, recording technicians, dramaturgs, camera operators, and so on, even before we take into account the promoters, audiences, reviewers and critics. And after the work is finished and ready to be made public, it cannot be recognised as legitimate art until it has been approved by the 'gatekeepers': art museums and curators, publishers and critics, established film or theatre companies, arts administrators and government arts departments, among others. In their control of what is 'legitimate' art, these gatekeepers also effectively say who is, and who is not, a legitimate artist.

Bourdieu is interested in how 'the artist' is defined and understood because it is a social effect, and a sociological 'problem'—the problem of how to define and position workers who are not really workers, thinkers who are not really scholars, disinterested agents who, if we study them a little more closely (as we pointed out in Chapter 8), are in fact deeply 'interested'. What Bourdieu does is to look at artists *relationally*, asking to what other fields, institutions, discourses and practices they are connected. He also looks at artists and art discourses *reflexively*, asking about the conditions that ensure artists will take up a particular social position, and people in the society will generally accept the charismatic stories about this position, despite all the evidence to the contrary. In asking these sorts of questions, he attempts to make sense of what attracts people to the field; because it certainly is not the money (art is a notoriously low-paid profession), and most artists would claim that fame is not the spur either—that they make their art 'for art's sake'.

Let us pick up the idea we discussed in the previous chapter, that the field of cultural production is divided between heteronomous (market-driven) and autonomous (art for art's sake) principles of production. This does not apply just to the discourses, the principles of production and the products themselves—it also applies to the artists. And the bifurcated nature of the field brings up another sociological problem, because if we define artists as being transcendent, romantic and disinterested, then what do we make of those artists who work at the heteronomous pole of the field? Are they 'not really artists'? Yet if commercial work is as much part of the field as 'pure' art (albeit less consecrated), then the people who make that work must also be 'real artists'. Now the definition of artists as charismatic begins to fall apart, and instead we start to see it as a manufactured category, one which exists for particular reasons—or 'interests': the interest of established artists and other gatekeepers in controlling the field. So although all artists are deeply invested in the social and economic field, Bourdieu argues that the charismatic conception of the artist remains a dominant view because it is in the interests of dominant agents in the field.

Positions in the field

There are a number of positions available within the field of cultural production, from the purely commercial at one end, to the purely aesthetic at the other. All the positions are, to a greater or lesser extent, committed to the field's principles of evaluation and practice, and all practitioners within that field will be familiar with dominant artistic discourses. So it is important not to think of the field as structured in a flat linear fashion, with aesthetics at one end, economics at the other, and practitioners distributed in between. Bourdieu has drawn up a much more complex, multi-dimensional model of the field (1990c: 96, 1993c: 49), one that distributes positions not only according to whether work is autonomous with respect to the social and economic fields, but by considering a whole range of other principles—forms, styles, media, the degree of 'consecration' claimed and the relation to artistic tradition.

The first organising principle is one of binary relations—a series of paired terms in which one term is privileged over the other: autonomous/heteronomous, art/craft, high art/popular culture, abstract/realist, contemporary/conventional, professional/ amateur. None of these terms is stable: today's high art may be tomorrow's popular culture. For instance, when classical music emerged as muzak in lifts and shopping centres, it immediately lost much of its symbolic value. But the terms, and the values attached to them, are used to organise and evaluate positions in the field, not just on a linear two-dimensional plane, but by taking into account the many other divisions and structures in the field.

Bourdieu's second organising principle is to divide the heteronomous pole between popular and commercial art. The commercial is art that is committed to the economic principle— industrial photography or television advertisements, for instance—while the 'popular' is committed to satisfying pre-established audiences—a John Grisham novel, or virtually any Hollywood film, for instance. He also divides the autonomous pole between the conventional (or authorised), and the avant garde. Conventional artists (he also calls them 'bourgeois' artists) work within current conventions. Examples of such artists could be the film director Stephen Spielberg, the painter David Hockney or the novelist Graham Greene, each of whom has consistently produced polished and compelling work in conventional media and without necessarily tilting at the windmills of artistic value. Bourdieu opposes them to what he calls the 'avant garde'—artists who do challenge established art practices and values. Examples might be the 'young British artists' (such as Damien Hirst, Rachel Whiteread and others whose works are in the Saatchi Collection), or the Americans Jeff Koons, Robert Mapplethorpe or Jenny Holzer. All these artists tend to reject established subject matter and media, and to test the limits of what can be defined as 'art'.

We have seen that Bourdieu establishes positions within the cultural field on the grounds of their relationship to the social and economic fields, and to artistic traditions and values. He describes, in *Photography* (see particularly pp. 95–8), a third organising principle for understanding positions available to artists. This one is related to form and media, and he calls it 'the principle of legitimation'. There are three levels of legitimation for Bourdieu. The first, the 'legitimate', includes consecrated forms such as music, plastic arts, literature or theatre, that are usually considered to be significant for all people, for all time—the sort of statements that are made about Mozart, Shakespeare, or da Vinci. The second, the 'legitimisable', includes works that lack the patina of high art, such as cinema, photography and jazz, but are still considered creative. Finally, 'arbitrary' practices are both commercial and popular—interior design, or fashion, for instance—and are legitimated from the commercial sector, by institutions and individuals such as designers or advertisers.

It is important to bear in mind that none of these positions, or principles for establishing positions, is stable or permanent. The same piece of work can go from being highly avant garde to very orthodox to popular and even to commercial, depending on the social and historical context, and how it is being used. In the previous chapter we mentioned the painter Edvard Munch, who began as an 'alienated' (avant garde) artist, but became more established until now it is *de rigueur* for major art museums to own a Munch. In other words, he became orthodox. But the uses to which his anguished painting *The Scream* has been put mean that he has also become popular ('everyone knows *The Scream*'), and even commercial—you can buy socks, coffee mugs and blow-up dolls printed with *The Scream* figure.

Similarly, the same work and artist can be positioned as legitimate, legitimisable or arbitrary, depending on temporal and perspectival position of the viewer. The New Zealand-born photographer/photojournalist Brian Brake is an example of this. Throughout the 1950s and 1960s he was taking photographs for news and feature journals like *Time Life* magazine and *Picture Post*—for generalist rather than artistic audiences. A non-reflexive application of Bourdieu's model of the field would note the circumstances under which his photographs were taken, and locate him in the heteronomous, arbitrary, commercial positions. But during this same period he was also a member of the prestigious freelance photography agency Magnum, working alongside photographic artists like Henri Cartier-Bresson and Ernst Haas; and many of his works have been acquired by state art museums and exhibited in significant venues. Viewed from this perspective, and with the benefit of history—so that we can see how he has been appropriated by the field of cultural production—he could as easily be classified as a 'real artist' (rather than a technician), and legitimate rather than legitimisable or arbitrary.

The point in describing this complex net of positions and possibilities is not to make the field hopelessly convoluted. Rather, what Bourdieu provides in his model is a 'plotting' of the field, and of the positions available therein. And it becomes useful to students of the field of cultural production because it shows that creative production does not occur in a vacuum. Artists make their work, and position it and themselves, according to what they see as possible and as being in their best interests at a given moment. And consequently, we can argue, art is not something made by a specially gifted individual, but is a commodity, a social product, made by someone who comes from a particular social background, and is working in a particular social context.

How the work and the artist are defined and categorised depends, as Bourdieu has pointed out, on the stories told about them, and the status (the 'capital') of the storytellers. The elderly man who is brought along to an art museum by his daughter, and complains that Georges Seurat's painting *Alfalfa Fields, Saint-Denis* (1885–86) is not much of a painting because virtually the whole canvas is filled with flowers and there is almost no view of Saint-Denis, has no field-based authority to say so, and consequently his evaluation will not be taken seriously. On the other hand, the director of a national museum who insists that, say, Damien Hirst is one of the greatest living artists, is likely to be able to influence how Hirst is viewed by the artistic and the general public.

The artistic habitus

While Bourdieu provides a carefully wrought model of the field and its institutions and discourses, what is missing in his earlier publications is what contemporary artists were actually saying and doing—his attention is focused on structures and audiences. He filled this gap with the publication of *Free Exchange*, an extended 'conversation' between himself and the New York-based visual artist Hans Haacke on contemporary art practice, and on the artistic habitus.

So, what disposes artists to take up, or compete for, one or other position? Bourdieu's answer is that it is the habitus, because this is the embodied structure that generates our ambitions, aspirations and dispositions. In making this point, he reinforces his insistence that the Romantic view of the artist we discussed earlier, and the notion that creativity is a special gift, are not valid. Rather, both the ability to be creative and the practice of being creative are effects of the combination of individual artists' habitus, and their social and historical contexts.

Think back to Chapter 2 where we discussed the concept of habitus. You will recall that the habitus develops out of the individual's history, including things like class origins, family background and educational opportunities. This is clearly the case for art: a central point, made by Bourdieu in virtually all his writings on artists, is that:

> Culture is a stake which, like all social stakes, simultaneously presupposes and demands that one take part in the game and be taken in by it, and interest in culture, without which there is no race, no competition, is produced by the very race and competition which it produces. The value of culture, the supreme fetish, is generated in the initial investment implied by the mere fact of entering the game. (1984: 250)

So the very act of participating in the field, as artist or as audience, 'proves' that it is important and, by extension, that the person participating in it has a shared value—which, of course, comes out of their own habitus. Someone, for instance, who grew up in a family where art was considered important, and where the family members were knowledgeable about, and comfortable with, art will have been continually exposed to art and to information about art; will have been imbued with the notion that art is important; and will be able, without thinking about it, to make the sort of statements and moves that display their own 'feel for the game'. Such a person never has to try to show their distinction, or even to think about it; it appears natural both to that person and to others. By contrast, someone who does not have these sorts of deeply installed knowledges and dispositions will not have that 'feel for the game'. But if that person is conscious of lacking—and aspires to possess—such markers of distinction, he or she will have to work at attaining them, and will be likely to be seen by those who already possess the artistic habitus as a newcomer, a *dilettante*, or a 'try-hard'. Habitus is important in making sense of what artists do and how they understand themselves and their field, because artists compete for, and take up, positions on the basis of two important structures: the *objective* structures (the field and its institutions) which make positions available; and the *incorporated* structures (the habitus), which predispose individuals to enter the field.

Let us look first at the incorporated structures, which include individual artists' general social position. This is, perhaps, the more important precondition for how artists, or potential artists, will 'play the game' of art. The more capital individuals already possess, the more likely it is that they will have the confidence to compete, and to assume that they are likely to succeed—an assumption that is often fulfilled.

There are two reasons for this 'winner takes all' perspective. The first is that if someone already possesses capital (whether symbolic, social, cultural or economic), they are more likely to have the experience, the cash, the skills and the social contacts to strategise their moves in a way that is likely to guarantee them success. Bruce Wayne/Batman is an example of this. In his dual identity, he is wealthy, intelligent, socially important and sophisticated, and at the same time, alert to 'the criminal mind' and skilled at kicking, punching and using complicated anti-crime devices. Using his money, social capital and cultural capital (in both business and criminal milieux), he can strategise his moves in both worlds, and is remarkably successful in both.

The second reason is that if someone is generally successful, or from a valued social background, other people are likely to assume that they will succeed in almost anything else they might undertake, and to support them in their undertakings. Think of the way in which celebrities are called on to raise funds for charities—Sting for rainforests, or Bob Geldof for African famine victims, for instance. Although they may have had no expertise relevant to the organisation they were supporting, and hence no formal authority to speak for that organisation, the capital they possessed as successful musicians and celebrities legitimated them to be spokespeople, and their success is a matter of public record.

The other basis for artistic practice is the objective structures in which artists are operating—in other words, the field and its institutions. Although Bourdieu insists that it is not possible to analyse this objective 'field of positions' without at the same time analysing the 'field of position-takings' (what people actually do in the field), it is the field of positions that tends to dominate practice. This is because once people enter a field, their habitus begins to take on the values and norms of that field, and to generate dispositions to think, act and believe in ways that are approved by the field. In the field of cultural production, for instance, the dominant theme is of the value of the aesthetic.

This is so much the case that even artists who are employed to work on a commercial basis—designing magazine covers, for instance—will reproduce this discourse of aesthetic value, despite the fact that under it, their own (commercial) practice is coded as inferior.

What this seems to suggest is that we can talk about an 'artistic habitus', and identify consistent dispositions and behaviours in the lives of people who identify themselves as artists. Certainly there are 'artistic types' that most of us could cite, if called on; particular ways of dressing, for instance (colourful and eccentric clothing); a commitment to the inner life and to a personal vision (being moody and eccentric); having an attitude of disinterest in 'normal' measures of success (like bank balances, or a large mortgage); and, of course, a 'bohemian' lifestyle (distanced from bourgeois respectability). While these are simply stereotypes that are not necessarily the experience of a great many artists, they are stereotypes that dominate the popular imagination—and the popular representation of artists.

Artists, in other words, are considered to be autonomous with respect to the status quo or to general social norms. Because they are 'not like' the 'rest of us', they do not have to obey the usual rules that stipulate what it means to be an adult member of society—holding down a steady job, paying off a mortgage, marrying and raising children, or being on time for appointments (though of course many of them do in fact hold down jobs, pay off mortgages and maintain conventional family lives). The 'artistic lifestyle' is often associated with extreme, and sometimes self-destructive behaviour. Think, for instance, of Jackson Pollack's or Dylan Thomas' excessive drinking; of Pablo Picasso's or Norman Mailer's sexual proclivities; of the 'junkie poets' (Coleridge, Byron) of the nineteenth century; or the 'junkie artists' of the twentieth century (Janis Joplin, Brett Whiteley). This 'wild child' aspect of the artistic habitus has also been popularised in film. In *Amadeus*, for instance, Mozart was represented as both musical genius and irresponsible; Jean-Michel Basquiat and Andy Warhol were portrayed in *Basquiat* as eccentric in behaviour, and extreme in social and sexual relations; and *Love is the Devil* showed the artist Francis Bacon as selfish, erratic and sexually 'perverse'. In other words, there is a popular notion that artists are different from the rest of us, and that their artistic genius in some way authorises their 'bad' behaviour.

Habitus and social action

Bourdieu also refers to artists as 'heterodoxical' because of the freedom they claim from social norms. What he means by this is that just as the 'orthodox' work to maintain the status quo, so the 'heterodox' actively work against the status quo. This should mean that artists, being scandalous and even revolutionary in their lifestyle and attitude to general norms of respectability, would be agents of sociopolitical action. But curiously, this is not necessarily the case. Hans Haacke discusses this in his 'conversation' with Bourdieu. He identifies, as a feature of the artistic habitus, an awareness that artistic production is a mode of a political expression; and as a second, somewhat contradictory feature, the fact that artists are not easy to mobilise in political action. This is, he suggests, because they are committed to individuality and free expression. While they recognise that there are limits on that free expression (in the shape of formal and informal forms of censorship), they cannot easily resist such constraints because 'Artists aren't organizers. They hate bureaucracy and meetings. It bores them' (in Bourdieu 1995: 12).

Consequently, a significant aspect of the artistic habitus—at least as Haacke describes it—is that the disposition to produce works is accompanied by a certain incapacity to engage effectively in the wider social, economic and political fields. This is not really surprising. Just as 'good art' has to be presented as though it is 'disinterested', 'good artists' have to appear to be 'disinterested', which means it is not easy for them to engage in direct political action. In fact, there is something of a contradictory set of dispositions in the artistic habitus: on the one hand, to challenge society; and on the other, to focus on the aesthetic, rather than the political aspect of their work. This means that the artistic habitus cannot easily accommodate both political engagement and artistic disinterestedness.

Habitus and disinterestedness

Disinterestedness is one of the most significant markers of artistic identity. We discussed in the previous chapter the way in which the field of cultural production values distance from the tackiness of economic necessity, or the banality of social necessity. Because of this attitude, artists are often seen as innocents—the film *Basquiat* again serves as an example, where Jean-Michel Basquiat is artistically brilliant, but a social naif—he does not know how to play the 'game' of commercial artistic success, which inevitably destroys him. This is a story that is repeated over and over in representations of the lives of artists. Caught between the 'intrinsic necessity' of the work of art—what their habitus drives them to do—and the social pressures that limit what can be said, goes the story, the artist's 'soul' is eaten up.

Bourdieu resists the temptation to romanticise the artistic habitus. Instead, he points out, successful artists are competent professionals who strategically assess what they will make, and where they will present their work, in the interests of maximising their own gain—whether measured in economic, symbolic or social terms (1995: 11). The American short story writer Raymond Carver is a prime example of this. Although we can assume that he approached his work as an artist, with his own vision and aesthetic, media reports during the late 1990s indicate that he gave over considerable autonomy to his editor. The editor claimed in those reports to have substantially rewritten Carver's stories, with Carver's agreement; an instance, presumably, of an artist making a strategic decision about what he needed to give up in the interests of gaining more sales, more symbolic capital, or perhaps closer editorial attention.

Bourdieu identifies this sort of strategic compliance with the demands of institutions and gatekeepers not as naïveté, but as a (perhaps unconscious) calculation, the ability to anticipate what is happening and make strategic moves, which is another feature of the artistic habitus. Because most artists are dependent for financial support on government grants, institutional sponsorship or their employers, they tend to practise a form of self-censorship. After all, even at the most autonomous pole of the field of cultural production we have witnessed, during the 1990s, the cancellation of exhibitions considered to be offensive, the withdrawal of funds, and even prosecution for obscenity. In such a climate, artists are likely to learn how to balance the competing needs of social safety and maximum gain, with free expression and critical acclaim. 'Every expression,' Bourdieu writes, 'is an accommodation between an *expressive interest* and a *censorship* constituted by the field in which that expression is offered' (1993b: 90). In other words, an important feature of the artistic habitus is the ability to make these sort of accommodations, while still satisfying the demands of the field of cultural production.

Artistic capital

This brings us back to the issue of capital, or what it is that constitutes 'gain' for artists. You will recall that 'capital' for Bourdieu means any sort of resource, including intangibles such as expertise, social networks, or prestige. And it takes various forms: Bourdieu lists economic, social, symbolic, or cultural capital. We pointed out earlier that the field of cultural production tends to regard economic capital as 'tacky'. But at the same time, we argued, the field of cultural production does depend on the economic field, because artworks have to be distributed and publicised; and also because artists have to buy food and pay bills just like everyone else. This means that it is not possible to hold a true distance from economic necessity, or to take risks in art-making, unless one has a source of income that provides this sort of freedom—being either independently wealthy, or supported by the wealthy.

Artists are rarely 'the wealthy'; in fact, the field of cultural production offers notoriously low incomes. Rather, artists are what Bourdieu calls 'the dominated of the dominant' because they 'possess all the properties of the dominant class *minus one*: money' (1993c: 165). What this means is that artists have to turn themselves into commodities, so that they can trade the symbolic capital they represent for a way of making a living.

One of the ways in which artists can commoditise themselves is by assuming an exotic quality. We mentioned earlier that some of the features of the artistic habitus include a tendency to develop a volatile, colourful and eccentric lifestyle, and this is one way of commoditising the self—being sufficiently different (through a sort of brand recognition) so that you are seen as exciting and valuable, and as something associated with distinction. Where artists market themselves as something of value, and something to be desired, they can be defined as commodities. This is a dangerous path for an artist, because the moment their performance is seen to be just that—an act, rather than an inherent difference—they lose authenticity and value.

The Australian pianist David Helfgott is an example—perhaps unwittingly—of this. In the decade or so prior to *Shine*, the 1997 Academy-award winning movie of his life, Helfgott was performing fairly regularly but in a low-key manner. After *Shine*, he became immensely popular, partly because of his character as it was portrayed in the movie—fragile, eccentric, a little strange—and people who were not usually concert-goers flocked to his performances. This backfired, artistically, because the critics reviewing his 1997 tour of the United States were highly abrasive, positioning him not as a 'real artist' but as a commodity, a kind of 'freak show' produced by Hollywood. There was a heated debate between critics, concert-goers and other concert pianists, which gradually died down, and Helfgott continues to perform to some critical and substantial popular success. In fact, by 1999 he had released several CDs, performed successfully in concerts around the world, raised money for charities, and gradually raised his own artistic profile—recommoditising himself as artist rather than 'just' a celebrity.

Conclusion

Bourdieu's attention to art and the field of cultural production has been a largely successful attempt to break with the intellectual bias that dominates the analysis of artistic practice. Instead, what he does is to regard aesthetic knowledge and practice as 'a particular and privileged case of practical knowledge . . . to create a theory of practice *as practice*' (1993a: 267). This process demystifies the world of art and artists, tests the discourses of genius, of privilege, of disinterestedness, and explores how art is used in society. In this process Bourdieu provides the tools not only to map out the cultural field, but to find ways of resisting its being deployed in the reproduction of social inequities.

In this chapter we have:

- traced the ways in which the identity of 'the artist' is formulated, and shown the problems associated with the notion that artists are charismatically alienated, or particularly gifted geniuses;
- detailed the various positions available within the field of cultural production;
- described the artistic habitus as a feel for the game (of cultural production) that depends on, and develops out of, individual artists' own backgrounds and the social contexts in which they are practising; and
- discussed the way in which competition within the field, and discourses about the field, may be used to maintain social inequities by presenting 'cultivated tastes' as not only natural, but more valuable than 'popular (vulgar) tastes'.

Further reading

Bourdieu, Pierre and Hans Haacke 1995, *Free Exchange*, Polity Press, Cambridge, pp. 68–100

Jenkins, Richard 1992, *Pierre Bourdieu*, Routledge, London and New York, Ch 6

Robbins, Derek 1991, *The Work of Pierre Bourdieu: Recognizing Society*, Open University Press, Milton Keynes, Ch 8

Staniszewski, Mary Anne 1995, *Believing is Seeing: Creating the Culture of Art*, Penguin, Harmondsworth, Ch 10

10

Journalism and television

In Chapters 8 and 9 we looked at Bourdieu's work on, and his theorising of, the general field of cultural production and the specific sub-field of art. These fields are given a great deal of emphasis by Bourdieu largely because their practitioners are 'holders of the (quasi) monopoly of the instruments of diffusion' (1998c: 1). That is to say, as producers of 'culture' they are, at the same time, producers of the different ideas, world views, discourses and meanings that largely determine what can and cannot be thought and done in a society.

It was Nietzsche who made the point that meaning is always first and foremost the result of political struggles, and that dominant groups always try to exercise control over what meanings are generally available or privileged. In texts such as *Practical Reason* and *On Television*, Bourdieu argues that in contemporary society culture undertakes precisely this function:

> Culture is unifying: the state contributes to the unification of
> the cultural market by unifying all codes, linguistic and
> juridical, and by effecting a homogenization of all forms of
> communication . . . Through classification systems . . .
> inscribed in law, through bureaucratic procedures, educational
> structures and social rituals . . . the state molds mental
> structures and imposes common principles of vision and
> division . . . And it thereby contributes to the construction of

what is commonly designated as national identity.
(1998d: 45–6)

Our earlier references to the field of cultural production concentrated very much on what Bourdieu calls the sub-field of 'restricted production', which involves (capital-C) Cultural forms such as literature, classical music and 'serious' art. As we have seen, this sub-field has two main characteristics: it is relatively autonomous and, as a corollary, it usually sets greater value in cultural than in economic capital. The other sub-field, which Bourdieu calls the field of large-scale production:

> involves what we sometimes refer to as 'mass' or 'popular' culture: privately owned television, most cinematic productions, radio . . . Sustained by a large and complex culture industry, its dominant principle of hierarchization involves economic capital or 'the bottom line'. Its very nature and its dependence on the broadest possible audience makes it less susceptible to formal experimentation. (1993b: 16)

Collaboration between practitioners in the field of cultural production (artists, intellectuals, academics—and journalists) is central to what we might call Bourdieu's political program, which is 'to universalize the conditions of access to the universal' (1998c: 1). And theoretically, practitioners from the sub-field of restricted (artistic) production, particularly those working in the media, would be expected to play a significant role in this program, precisely because the cultural texts they produce are associated with or reach mass audiences. As Bourdieu writes: 'Television enjoys a de facto monopoly on what goes into the heads of a significant part of the population and what they think' (1998c: 18).

And yet Bourdieu has devoted very little space, in his work on the field of cultural production (books such as *The Field of Cultural Production, The Rules of Art, The Love of Art* and *Distinction*) to the role of the media in these fields; or, more generally, to the part they play as disseminators of meaning. Two of his later works, *The Weight of the World* and *On Television*, do confront these issues to some extent, but in a way which seems to leave very little room for the likelihood of journalists working to 'universalise the conditions of access to the universal'. In order to understand why Bourdieu effectively writes off what is clearly a politically significant sector of the field of cultural production, we need to look, in some detail, at how Bourdieu understands the work of culture within the field of journalism, the extent to which it is influenced or determined by the field of power and the market, and the relation between television and journalism.

Journalism as a field

Bourdieu understands journalism as a split field that has always been informed, at least theoretically, by the characteristics of the poles of both restricted and large-scale production:

> The journalistic field emerged as such during the nineteenth century around the opposition between newspapers offering 'news', preferably 'sensational' or better yet, capable of creating a sensation, and newspapers featuring analysis and 'commentary', which marked their difference from the other group by loudly proclaiming the values of 'objectivity'. Hence, this field is the site of an opposition between two models, each with its own principle of legitimation: that of peer recognition, accorded individuals who internalize most completely the internal 'values' or principles of the field; or that of recognition by the public at large, which is measured by numbers of readers, listeners, or viewers, and therefore, in the final analysis, by sales and profits. (1998c: 70)

But overall, the field of journalism describes itself, justifies its activities, and predicates its value to the community, in terms of what we can call 'autonomous principles'. These principles, which are usually articulated in a professional code of ethics, often include a commitment to truth, accuracy and freedom of speech, the public's right to know, unbiased reporting and independence. Theoretically these principles should inform and even dictate all aspects of the journalist's work, including what should constitute news, how it is reported and gathered, and whose opinions are sought and authorised.

For Bourdieu, a field or sub-field is made up of governing bodies, rules and regulations, and languages which both influence practitioners and evaluate their activities. Practitioners in the field of journalism have many possibilities to choose from (from which angle to write a story, what questions to ask in an interview), but they know their actions will be judged by the field, its standards and values. This is true of all practitioners in the field(s) of journalism—even such powerful media magnates as Rupert Murdoch, Conrad Black, Silvio Berlusconi and Ted Turner.

At the very least the *performance* of a commitment to both the principles of the field (the public's right to know, reporting without fear or favour) and its capital (a good reputation, the respect of one's peers) is required from practitioners in the field of journalism—something which is the case with all the fields associated with the sub-field of restricted production. But, as Bourdieu points out, journalism differs from fields such as art and the academy in one important respect: 'it is much more dependent on external forces than the other fields of cultural production . . . It depends very directly on demand since . . . it is subject to the decrees of the market and the opinion poll' (1998c: 53). In other words, because newspapers, television stations and other media are run predominantly as businesses, the bottom line for any cultural text produced by journalists is whether or not it has a market, and is economically viable.

Journalism and the market

This transformation of the field of journalism by the market has, for Bourdieu, four major consequences. First, while the field and its practitioners theoretically adhere to the rule of cultural capital as it applies within the field of restricted production, in practice this is frequently not the case. Bourdieu considers that, 'the journalistic field has no equivalent of the sort of immanent justice in the scientific world that censures those individuals who break certain rules and rewards those who abide by them with the esteem of their peers' (1998c: 53).

184

Breaking or abiding by rules, writing ill-informed or intelligently analytical articles, being ignored or cited by other journalists—all this means very little in terms of the wider field's own ethical discourses and imperatives. Rather, the bottom line is usually 'Will this sell?' Journalists regularly engage in practices that can be considered at best exploitative and ethically dubious, and at worst a breach of the law; examples involving UK newspapers in 2001 included the so-called 'entrapment' of Sophie Rhys-Jones, the listing of the names and addresses of convicted paedophiles and the publication of an interview that effectively caused the trial of two prominent English soccer players to be aborted. But while these activities may produce some negative consequences for the paper and their journalists (the Queen may not be amused; fines may be levied; and journalists can, in theory, be jailed), the 'scandal' of their transgression doesn't necessarily translate into negative capital within the field, either for the paper or for the journalists involved. In fact, the adage that there is 'no such thing as bad publicity' is particularly appropriate with regard to most areas of the field of journalism; to paraphrase Oscar Wilde, 'the only thing that would be worse than the public and the media talking and writing about you . . . was if they weren't talking and writing about you'.

The second consequence of market domination of the field, according to Bourdieu, is a lack of accountability. What this means is that newspaper and television journalists can provide accounts of, or make predictions about, public sphere matters such as elections (the November 2000 Bush–Gore election, which we discuss below, being a good case in point), government policies, strikes, demonstrations, economic trends or foreign affairs; but those accounts or predictions are never called to account (for instance, by other journalists). Bourdieu refers to this as:

> the prediction game, made possible by a collective amnesia about current events. Not only are these predictions and diagnoses easy to make (like bets on sports events) but they can be made with total impunity, protected as the predictor is by the rapidity with which the journalistic report is forgotten amid the rapid turnover of events. (1998c: 6)

Bourdieu's point is that the accuracy or acuity of reports is, in a sense, irrelevant. What matters is the extent to which they 'create' headlines, or sensationalise events. Bourdieu cites the example of the way the media hailed and celebrated the advent of democracy in eastern Europe, only to virtually write off much of the area as being caught up in, and defined by, endemic tribalism. This capricious approach also characterised the coverage of the American presidential primaries in 1999–2000. Very little attention was given, by any of the media, to issues that might differentiate the candidates (and what this might mean for the electorate), or even to the two clear front runners, Al Gore (Democrat) and George Bush (Republican). Each day, stories would be written which identified or dismissed candidates as presidential contenders; only to be revised or forgotten when the result of the latest primary or opinion poll was released. Further, most of the attention centred on human interest aspects of outsiders such as Bill Bradley (Democrat) and John McCain (Republican). Neither had any real hope of winning, but they were charismatic, went out of their way to cultivate the media and made for interesting stories. By the end of the primaries readers and viewers knew a great deal more about the men who wouldn't be running for president than they did about Gore and Bush and their policies. And of course when it came to the election itself, the US media were so keen to get the results out quickly that they got various results wrong, and may have inadvertently brought about some results by influencing voters to stay away from the polls because of their claim that the outcome was already decided.

The third consequence of market domination of journalism is what Bourdieu calls the censorship of the news. This takes three forms: political censorship, self-censorship and economic censorship (1998c: 15). Political censorship occurs, for instance, when governments make political appointments to senior public broadcasting management positions, or introduce policies which directly or indirectly threaten the independence of public broadcasters (for example, by forcing them to take advertisements to cover costs, or by tieing their funding to their ratings). Self-censorship is the result of the relative scarcity of jobs in the media, and the perception that media bosses can and will intervene if journalists don't toe the line. The result is that 'consciously or unconsciously, people censor themselves—they don't need to be called into line' (1998c: 15). Finally, links between media organisations and other business interests contribute to what Bourdieu calls 'economic censorship'. 'It's important', he writes:

> to know that NBC is owned by General Electric (which means that interviews with people who live near a nuclear power plant undoubtedly would be . . . but then again, such a story wouldn't even occur to anyone), that CBS is owned by Westinghouse, and ABC by Disney . . . and that these facts lead to consequences through a whole series of mediations. (1998c: 16)

The fourth, and in a sense the most significant, of the effects of economic domination is what Bourdieu calls 'the homogenising' of the field. Theoretically, the competition between journalism organisations and practitioners, driven by economic imperatives, might be expected to produce greater diversity (for instance in the genres employed, the versions and content of the news, the level of analysis, and the people who are quoted and interviewed as 'authorities'). Bourdieu claims, however, that competition produces a very different effect: 'rather than automatically generating originality and diversity, competition tends to favour uniformity. This can easily be verified by comparing the contents of the major weekly magazines, or radio and television stations aimed at a general audience' (1998c: 72–3). The reason for this is that once something (a story, an interview, a celebrity) has been identified as newsworthy by one organisation, everyone else feels obliged to follow suit, or suffer the consequences (loss of ratings or readership). Bourdieu's point is that there is an almost hysterical aspect to journalism's efforts to avoid the perception of having missed out or of being behind with regard to the news.

An excellent example of this occurred during the Bill Clinton/Monica Lewinsky scandal. Because the journalists were competing not only with traditional news media but also with the Internet (which first published Lewinsky's testimony to the

Starr enquiry), journalists produced a seemingly endless supply of 'takes' on the affair: Lewinsky was 'psychoanalysed', her health (and particularly her weight) became the subject of discussion and analysis, she was offered money to tell her exclusive story, her friends were sought out and interviewed and there was speculation about the extent of her sexual attractiveness (at one point she was dubbed the 'tubby temptress').

This process applies not only to celebrity stories and scandals, but to more overtly political and public sphere stories as well. Ethnic cleansing in eastern Europe, globalisation, political instability in Africa, Islamic terrorism: all these issues were picked up by virtually every journalism organisation at the same time, 'done to death', and then discarded as if they ceased to exist or hold any further significance. A recall of these issues is always possible, however, but only if enough newspapers or television programs decide they are newsworthy again.

Television, time and sensationalism

Although Bourdieu holds out the possibility, at the beginning of *On Television*, of collaborative political action involving journalists and other practitioners from the field of cultural production (1998c: 1), there is little in his description and analysis of the field to suggest how this might come about. Central to Bourdieu's dismissal of the field is his argument that not only is journalism dominated, to its detriment, by the market, but also that the more serious, reflective and analytical areas of the field—for instance, 'quality' newspapers and journals, and public broadcasters—are being inexorably transformed by the force of competition from, and the example of, commercial television.

To a large extent the major theme of *On Television* is the ways and the extent to which the medium of television, and in particular the conditions under which it produces news, information and debate, have made it increasingly difficult for journalists to undertake analysis or considered evaluation of it. In Bourdieu's view, commercial television programmes are circuses dominated by the twin constraints of 'time' and 'effect'. Time, for Bourdieu, is the biggest problem. He makes the point that the very limited time available to 'do' a story means that issues have to be pared back, decontextualised and explicated in terms of simple binaries (right/wrong, business/unions, men/women, citizens/foreigners).

News programmes provide the best example of this process. Stories which are connected to one another only in the sense that they happened at the same time (a famine in Africa, a celebrity divorce, the enactment of government policies) are thrown together in an order which is not so much arbitrary as interest driven ('Are people tired of hearing about African famines?'), without explanations of their contexts or antecedents. Moreover, because each event is dealt with in a minute or so, the explanation of the story has to be both punchy and evoke human interest (for instance, a famine might be articulated in terms of the plight of one starving child or family, or a government policy might be reduced to the effects of the policy on a single shopkeeper).

These twin imperatives of time and effect make it virtually impossible for news programmes to say anything that is not sensationalised or simplistic. In fact it really doesn't make sense for them to say anything much at all, which is why the news is invariably dominated by visuals. A 30-second description of a massacre, famine, riot or war strains to have an immediate emotional effect—what it is meant to accomplish. Film of a person being beaten to death, of emaciated babies, of crowds destroying buildings, or of bombs zeroing in on bridges or enemy troops takes the viewer into the story, and can provoke an immediate, and strong, response (pity, anger, fear, revulsion, elation).

This process does not just apply to television footage, but to visuals in general. An example of the way in which a photograph can come to set the agenda for the way an issue is discussed and understood occurred during the recent tug-of-war over the Cuban boy Elian Gonzalez between his Miami relatives and his father, who was still in Cuba. The dramatic photograph of a Florida state trooper who appeared to be pointing his rifle at the boy and one of the relatives (in fact this was an optical illusion, but that hardly mattered) became the issue, and dominated both television news and newspaper reports, commentaries and editorials.

Contextualising details (for instance, the fact that the authorities had been carrying out fruitless negotiations with the relatives, who threatened to use firearms to defend the boy); the physical and psychological welfare of Elian Gonzalez (who had been subjected to extraordinary stress and pressure by his relatives, the whole Miami-Cuban community and the press); the rights of the father (whose son was being illegally kept from him); and the political ramifications of the issue (an influential community group could effectively defy the law, threaten to use weapons against the authorities and still attract the support of both presidential candidates and large sections of the Republican party, as well as prominent actors and singers)—all these aspects were effectively edited out of the story. Journalists opted instead to show, analyse, describe and solicit community responses to the photograph. The violence done to Elian Gonzalez (particularly by the press) and his father (by the Miami relatives and American politicians) lost out to the immediate emotive violence produced by the photograph.

Bourdieu argues that this dramatising and sensationalising effect of television news is passed on to the rest of the field because of the homogenising effect of competition and, more specifically, because of the high level of diffusion of commercial television. Television creates the templates and sets the agendas for what comes to be understood and treated as the news by newspapers and journals, which severely restricts what can and can't be thought and discussed. As Bourdieu writes: 'This sort of game of mirrors reflecting one another produces a formidable effect of mental closure' (1998c: 24).

Journalism and the field of cultural production

Bourdieu argues, in both *On Television* and *Acts of Resistance*, that market domination of journalism not only transforms that field; it also has two significant consequences for the field of cultural production. First, as we have seen, so-called 'quality journalism' practitioners and organisations are faced with the prospect of losing their cachet as they 'suffer under the pressure to make concessions to the market' (1998c: 73). And as the field of journalism becomes increasingly homogenised, its influence on other fields (particularly those structured in terms of the large-scale production model) passes on the trend of economic determinism and, as a corollary, the displacement of the hegemony of cultural capital. Bourdieu explains this transformation in terms of a practical politics of the field:

> Thus, the increased power of a journalistic field itself increasingly subject to direct or indirect domination by the market model threatens the autonomy of other fields of cultural production. It does so by supporting those actors or enterprises at the very core of those fields that are most inclined to yield to the seduction of 'external' profits precisely because they are less rich in capital specific to the field (scientific, literary, or other) and therefore less assured of the specific rewards the field is in a position to guarantee in the short or longer term. (1998c: 74)

We referred to this kind of politics in our discussion of the transformation of the field of sport in Chapter 2. While sport was always tied up with the market, this relationship was undeveloped and inconsistent. Certain sub-fields, such as golf and boxing, were strongly market oriented, while athletics, tennis and swimming were predominantly (and ostensibly) 'lily-white'. The changing of the guard in these sports (often manifested in the replacement, in senior organisational hierarchies, of elected amateur officials with appointed business managers) was facilitated by the media, both directly (through their campaigning for change, or by linking up with progressive officials or organisations) and indirectly (by giving increased, and positive, coverage to professional developments in the sport). Bourdieu's point about this 'politics of field' is best exemplified in the sports of cricket and rugby league, which were effectively taken over by businessmen with strong media interests (Kerry Packer, who set up and funded the breakaway World Series Cricket, and Rupert Murdoch in rugby league), and then put under the administrative control of officials or groups whose cultural capital and literacy was predominantly derived from the economic, media or legal, rather than the sporting, field.

This colonising of the field of cultural production by market forces (through the facilitation of the journalistic field) is of considerable political significance given the emphasis Bourdieu places on what he calls 'holders of the (quasi) monopoly of the instruments of diffusion' (1998c: 1). Those fields whose cultural capital is universally recognised or highly transposable (for example, the juridical field or the scientific field), or which traditionally have taken on the role of critically analysing the social doxa of the day (literature, art, intellectuals), are usually located at the restricted production pole of the field of cultural production and, accordingly, tend to provide an alternative perspective to the hegemony of the market. But journalism, given its particular self-professed role as a contemporary public sphere, has the power to potentially shift the juridical, scientific and other politically important fields towards the market; or simply to serve as an arm of the field of power in unifying and homogenising society. As Bourdieu writes:

> The journalistic field tends to reinforce the 'commercial'
> elements at the core of all fields to the detriment of the 'pure'.
> It favors those cultural producers most susceptible to the
> seduction of economic and political powers, at the expense of
> those intent on defending the principles and the values of
> their professions. (1998c: 70)

Journalism and the public sphere

Bourdieu's work on television and the field of journalism may seem overly pessimistic, almost akin to a Frankfurt School-style denunciation of mass culture. After all, there are many ways in which journalism and even television can be, and are, used to counter social doxa and the hegemony of the market and its discourses. For instance, most of the text of *On Television* is taken from two televised lectures given by Bourdieu on his terms—that he had control over content and time.

Bourdieu's argument, however, is that the capacity of the field of journalism to take on a genuine 'public sphere' function is dependent on it, first, remaining relatively free to take seriously its core principles, values and imperatives (a commitment to the public interest, unbiased reporting); and, second, on maintaining the ability to provide informed critical analyses of social, political and cultural issues. And for Bourdieu neither of these is possible if the field goes the way of television and its market-driven sensationalism.

What hope does Bourdieu hold, then, that the field of journalism and, more generally, the field of cultural production (and groups connected to this field, such as 'intellectuals'), can contribute to the project of universalising 'the conditions of access to the universal' (1998c: 1). His evaluation of the extent to which, and the ways in which, the field can contribute to this project in the face of impediments brought about by the domination of the market and television is exemplified in an appendix to *On Television*, titled 'The Olympics—an agenda for analysis'.

Bourdieu points out that the Olympic movement is, at least discursively, a 'gigantic spectacle of sport in which athletes from all over the world compete under the sign of universalistic ideals' (1998c: 79). What he calls here the 'hidden referent' is the way in which these ideals (bringing sportspeople from all over the world together to compete equally, promoting international trust and understanding) are transformed by the market and the field of journalism into both a 'war by other means' and a vast commercial enterprise (both of which pay nothing but lip service to Olympic ideals). In other words, the games have been taken from the participants and sold to the market. He posits that the only way to reverse this trend is for the participants 'to control the mechanisms that affect them all' (1998c: 81).

But how could this happen? After all, athletes are themselves caught up in a variety of political and commercial networks (through the policies of national associations, sports clubs and organisations, their ties with agents and sponsors, their roles in the field of journalism) that would seem effectively to preclude any move to reclaim collectively shared control of the movement and its ideals.

Resisting the market

Recent experiences in the field of sport (and elsewhere), however, would seem to suggest that Bourdieu does have a point here. An excellent example is the agonistics that have surrounded the attempts—by senior administrators, media owners and business in general—to corporatise Australian Rules Football. This sport has always had a strong tribal aspect to it, and has tended to think of itself (this applies to most players, club administrators, spectators and, interestingly enough, to most journalists) as 'the people's game'. Attempts to update the game by introducing better business procedures (advanced bookings for seating), corporate-friendly, high-tech stadiums and match scheduling that favoured television and other innovations were greeted with almost universal disapproval (crowds dropped off, players, coaches and administrators complained and journalists lambasted the changes). The alienation of the sport by the market and television has been strongly (and to a certain extent successfully) resisted, even by some members of the 'mechanisms of alienation' (journalists, lawyers and entrepreneurs). The same scenario is being played out, with minor variations, all over the world (in England with the opposition to Rupert Murdoch's take-over of Manchester United soccer team; in the USA with the community-owned Green Bay Packers and the re-born Cleveland Browns American football teams; and in international test cricket with the universal reaction against corruption of the game by bookmakers).

What are the mechanisms which allow people to resist the seduction of television and the market, in sport and elsewhere? Bourdieu's argument is that as sport and other cultural fields and institutions are alienated, members of those fields still retain, through the durability of the habitus, a strong commitment to the field's inalienable ideals, imperatives and values. It doesn't really matter whether these ideals are real or always inform practices (amateurism, fair play, reason, equality), or whether practitioners, to some extent, support these ideals in bad faith (because they possess the cultural capital that is tied up with, and dependent on, these ideals). They constitute perhaps the only practical basis of a resistance to the domination of the field of cultural production by the market, and the only alternative values—invariably articulated in terms of the 'reason' of universalising 'the conditions of access to the universal' (1998c: 1) to the discourse of economic rationalism.

This doesn't really overcome or address the objections raised by John Frow (and see Chapter 8) against Bourdieu's argument that fields or groups connected with the field of production, such as intellectuals, can 'stand in' as a universal field and thereby help to universalise access to the universal. But it does point to the way in which certain fields might feel the need to take on this role in order to work against the domination of their field (and the concomitant erosion or erasure of their cultural capital) by the market. As Bourdieu writes at the end of *Acts of Resistance:*

> if one can retain some reasonable hope, it is that, in state institutions and the dispositions of agents (especially those most attached to these institutions . . .), there still exists forces which, under the appearance of simply defending a vanishing order and the corresponding privileges . . . will . . . have to work to invent and construct a social order which is not governed solely by the pursuit of selfish interest and individual profit, and which makes room for collectives oriented towards rational pursuit of collectively defined and approved ends. (1998b: 104)

The media and political action

We suggested in Chapter 1 that Bourdieu saw his scholarly work as a means to an end; that is, as a commitment to the principle that although society is characterised by a politics of domination, inequality and endemic symbolic violence, 'what the social world has done, it can, armed with . . . knowledge, undo' (1999a: 629). Bourdieu's *On Television*, together with his other more openly politically interventionist texts (such as *Acts of Resistance* and *The Weight of the World*), constitutes a concerted effort on his part to 'reach beyond the usual audience at the Collège de France' (1998c: 10). Bourdieu has attempted to do this in a number of ways. The two lectures he gave about television were delivered on television, and were designed to get around the problems he associates with the media—trivialisation, sensationalism and the lack of time. Bourdieu gave his lectures via the audiovisual service of the Collège de France, and was not restricted with regard to time, topic or technical requirements. In his own words: 'I have a control of the instruments of production' (1998c: 13).

The book taken from the lectures was a bestseller in France, as was *The Weight of the World*. These texts, along with *Acts of Resistance*, provoked widespread debate, particularly in the media, about issues such as the market's domination of the public sphere, racism, social inequality, globalisation and the erosion of the welfare state. Of course Bourdieu was able to make these kinds of interventions precisely because of the considerable cultural capital he carries, particularly in France; a case of him learning from, and putting into practice, insights derived from his own body of theory.

Bourdieu also understands that although the media is dominated by commercial interests, and although its commitment to its own ethical imperatives and values (to serve the public interest, to act as a responsible public sphere) is an empty one, the existence of these values provides an opportunity for intellectuals to intervene in the public sphere.

How is this the case? In *Pascalian Meditations* Bourdieu writes about the sociolinguist P.H. Grice's maxims concerning the 'co-operative principle' of communication: 'Make your contribution such as is required, at the stage at which it occurs, by the accepted purpose or direction of the talk exchange in which you are engaged' (2000: 122). This principle, although 'constantly flouted', serves as:

> a kind of implicit presupposition of all conversation, a specific variant of the principle of reciprocity, which, although it is constantly transgressed, can be invoked at any time, as a reminder of the tacitly accepted rule or an implicit reference to what a conversation has to be in order to be a real dialogue. (2000: 122)

196

So although the game which is public sphere communication may be rigged (because commercial interests and dominant groups will always hold the trump cards), it has to 'perform up to its principles' if, in Bourdieu's term, the illusio of the game is to be maintained. This means being 'open' to the voices of all groups, but particularly groups, such as intellectuals, who have the cultural capital that allows them to speak on social issues such as racism or inequality with 'authority'.

Given this (potential) opening, intellectuals such as Bourdieu have an opportunity, and in a sense a duty, to effect some kind of transformation of the media-dominated public sphere. As Bourdieu writes:

> I would like writers, artists, philosophers and scientists to be able to make their voice heard directly in all the areas of public life in which they are competent. I think that everyone would have a lot to gain if the logic of intellectual life, that of argument and refutation, were extended to public life. At present, it is often the logic of political life, that of denunciation and slander, 'sloganization' and falsification of the adversary's thought, which extends into intellectual life. It would be a good thing if the 'creators' could fulfil their function of public service and sometimes public salvation (1998b: 9).

Conclusion

- Bourdieu has devoted very little space, in his work on the field of cultural production (books such as *The Field of Cultural Production*, *The Rules of Art*, *The Love of Art* and *Distinction*) to the role of the media in these fields; or more generally to the part they play as disseminators of meaning. Two of his later works, *The Weight of the World* and *On Television*, do confront these issues to some extent, but in a way which seems to leave very little room for the likelihood of journalists working to 'universalise the conditions of access to the universal'.
- Bourdieu understands journalism as a split field that has always been informed, at least theoretically, by the characteristics of the poles of both restricted and large-scale production.

197

- The conflict between discourse and practice in journalism is symptomatic of what Bourdieu would call a conflict of cultural capital within the field. While the field supposedly performs public sphere functions, and adheres to discourses of ethical and disinterested behaviour, at the same time it is also undeniably a business; and the capital, values and discourses of business are essentially antithetical to disinterestedness and ethical behaviour.

- Bourdieu argues that as sport and other cultural fields and institutions are alienated, members of those fields still retain, through the durability of the habitus, a strong commitment to the field's inalienable ideals, imperatives and values. This constitutes perhaps the only practical basis of a resistance to the domination of the field of cultural production by the market, and the only alternative values—invariably articulated in terms of the 'reason' of universalising 'the conditions of access to the universal' (1998c: 1)—to the discourse of economic rationalism.

Further reading

Bourdieu, Pierre 1998b, *Acts of Resistance*, Polity Press, Cambridge
Bourdieu, Pierre 1998c, *On Television*, New Press, New York

Bibliography

Works by Bourdieu

Note: Quotations from Bourdieu's works are referenced in the text by the publication date of the English edition.

——1958, *Sociologie de l'Algérie*, English edn 1962, *The Algerians*, trans. A.C.M. Ross, Beacon Press, Boston

——1972, *Esquisse d'un théorie de la pratique, précédé de trois études d'ethnologie kabyle*, English edn 1977a, *Outline of a Theory of Practice*, trans. R. Nice, Cambridge University Press, Cambridge

——1973, 'Cultural reproduction and social reproduction' in *Knowledge, Education and Cultural Change: Papers on the Sociology of Education*, ed. R. Brown, Tavistock, London, pp. 71–112

——1975, 'The specificity of the scientific field and the social conditions of the progress of reason' *Social Science Information*, 14/6, pp. 19–47

——1977, *Algérie soixante*, English edn 1979b, *Algeria 1960: The Disenchantment of the World, the Sense of Honour, The Kabyle House or the World Reversed*, trans. R. Nice, Cambridge University Press, Cambridge

——1978, 'Sport and social class' *Social Science Information*, 17/6, pp. 819–40

——1979, *La distinction. Critique sociale du jugement*, English edn 1984, *Distinction: A Social Critique of the Judgement of Taste*, trans. R. Nice, Routledge, London

——1979a, 'Public opinion does not exist' in *Communication and Class Struggle*, eds A. Mattelart and S. Siegelaub, International General, New York, pp. 124–30

——1980, *Le sens pratique*, English edn 1990b, *The Logic of Practice*, trans. R. Nice, Stanford University Press, Stanford

——1980, *Questions de sociologie*, English edn 1993b, *Sociology in Question*, Sage, London

——1981, 'Men and machines' in *Advances in Sociological Method and Methodology: Towards an Integration of Micro- and Macro-sociologies*, eds K. Knorr-Cetina and A.V. Cicourel, Routledge & Kegan Paul, Boston and London, pp. 304–17

——1982, *Ce que parler veut dire. L'économie des échanges linguistiques*, English edn 1991a, *Language and Symbolic Power*, ed. J.B. Thompson, trans. G. Raymond and M. Adamson, Polity Press, Cambridge

——1984, *Homo academicus*, English edn 1988a, *Homo Academicus*, trans. P. Collier, Polity Press, Cambridge

——1986a, 'An antinomy in the notion of collective protest' in *Development, Democracy and the Art of Trespassing*, eds A. Foxley, M.S. McPherson and G. O'Donnel, University of Notre Dame Press, Notre Dame, IN

——1986b, 'The struggle for symbolic order: interview with Honneth, Kacyba and Schwibs' *Theory, Culture and Society*, 3/3, pp. 35–51

——1987, 'What makes a social class? On the theoretical and practical existence of groups', trans. L. Wacquant and D. Young, *Berkeley Journal of Sociology*, pp. 1–17

——1987a, *Choses dites*, English edn 1990a, *In Other Words: Essays Towards a Reflexive Sociology*, trans. M. Adamson, Stanford University Press, Stanford, CT

——1988, *L'ontologie politique de Martin Heidegger*, English edn 1991b, *The Political Ontology of Martin Heidegger*, trans. P. Collier, Polity Press, Cambridge

——1989, *La noblesse d'état. Grandes écoles et esprit de corps*, English edn 1996a, *State Nobility: Elite Schools in the Field of Power*, trans. L.C. Clough, Polity Press, Cambridge

——1992, *Les règles de l'art. Genèse et structure du champ littéraire*, English edn 1996b, *The Rules of Art: Genesis and Structure of the*

Literary Field, trans. S. Emanuel, Stanford University Press, Stanford, CT

——1992a, 'Rites as acts of institution' in *Honor and Grace in Anthropology*, eds J.G. Peristiany and J. Pitt-Rivers, Cambridge University Press, Cambridge, pp. 79–89

——1992b, 'Thinking about limits' *Theory, Culture and Society*, 9/1, 37–49

——1993, 'Concluding remarks: for a sociogenetic understanding of cultural works' in *Bourdieu: Critical Perspectives*, eds C. Calhoun, E. LiPuma and M. Postone, Polity Press, Cambridge, pp. 263–75

——1993a, *The Field of Cultural Production: Essays on Art and Literature*, ed. and introd. R. Johnson, Polity Press, Cambridge

——1994, *Raisons pratiques. Sur la theorie de l'action*, English edn 1998d, *Practical Reason: On the Theory of Action*, Polity Press, Cambridge

——1994a, 'Rethinking the state: genesis and structure of the bureaucratic field' *Sociological Theory*, 12/1, pp. 1–18

——1996, *Sur la télévision*, English edn 1998c, *On Television*, trans. P.P. Ferguson, New Press, New York

——1997, *Méditations pascaliennes*, English edn 2000, *Pascalian Meditations*, trans. R. Nice, Polity Press, Cambridge

——1998, *Contre-feux. Propos pour servir à la résistance contre l'invasion néo-libérale*, English edn 1998b, *Acts of Resistance: Against the New Myths of Our Time*, trans. R. Nice, Polity Press, Cambridge

——1998a, *La domination masculine*, English edn 2001, *Masculine Domination*, trans. R. Nice, Stanford University Press, Stanford, CT

——and J.-C. Passeron 1964, *Les héritiers. Les étudiants et la culture*, English edn 1979, *The Inheritors: French Students and their Relations to Culture*, trans. Richard Nice, University of Chicago Press, Chicago

——with L. Boltanski, R. Castel, J.-C. Chamboredon and D. Schnapper 1965, *Un art moyen. Essais sur les usages sociaux de la photographie*, English edn 1990c, *Photography: A Middle-brow Art*, trans. S. Whiteside, Stanford University Press, Stanford, CT

——with J.-C. Passeron and M. de Saint Martin 1965, *Rapport pédagogique et communication*, English edn 1992c, *Academic Discourse: Linguistic Misunderstanding and Professional Power*, trans. R. Teese, Polity Press, Cambridge

——with J.-C. Chamboredon and J.-C. Passeron 1968, *Le métier de sociologue. Préalables épistémologiques*, English edn 1991c, *The Craft of Sociology: Epistemological Preliminaries*, ed. B. Krais, trans. R. Nice, Walter de Gruyter, New York

——and A. Darbel, with D. Schnapper 1969, *L'amour de l'art. Les musées d' art et leur public*, English edn 1991e, *The Love of Art: European Art Museums and their Public*, trans. C. Beattie and N. Merrium, Polity Press, Cambridge

——and J.–C. Passeron 1970, *La reproduction. Éléments pour une théorie du systéme d' enseignement*, English edn 1977b, *Reproduction in Education, Society and Culture*, trans. R. Nice, Sage, London

——and J.S. Coleman (eds) 1991d, *Social Theory for a Changing World*, Westview Press, Boulder, CO

——and L. Wacquant 1992, *Résponses. Pour une anthropologie réflexive*, English edn 1992a, *An Invitation to Reflexive Sociology*, Polity Press, Cambridge

——with A. Accardo et al. 1993, *La misère du monde*, English edn 1999a, *The Weight of the World: Social Suffering in Contemporary Society*, trans. P.P. Ferguson, Stanford University Press, Stanford, CT

——and H. Haacke 1994, *Libre-Échange*, English edn 1995, *Free Exchange*, trans. R. Johnson, Stanford University Press, Stanford, CT

——and T. Eagleton 1994a, 'Doxa and common life: an interview' in *Mapping Ideology*, ed. S. Zirek, Verso, London, pp. 265–77

——and L. Wacquant 1999b, 'On the cunning of imperialist reason' *Theory, Culture and Society*, 16/1, pp. 41–58

Other references

Appadurai, Arjun 1997, *Modernity at Large*, University of Minnesota Press, Minneapolis

Austin, J.L. 1962, *How to Do Things with Words*, Clarendon Press, Oxford

Bryson, Bill 1995, *Notes from a Small Island*, Doubleday, London, Sydney

Calhoun, Craig, Edward LiPuma and Moishe Postone (eds) 1993, *Bourdieu: Critical Perspectives*, Polity Press, Cambridge

Certeau, Michel de 1984, *The Practice of Everyday Life*, trans. Steven Rendall, University of California Press, Berkeley

Eagleton, Terry 1983, *Literary Theory: An Introduction*, Blackwell, Oxford

——1994, 'Ideology and its Vicissitudes in Western Marxism', in *Mapping Ideology*, ed. Slavoj Zizek, Verso, London, pp. 210–26

Foster, Arnold W. and Judith R. Blau (eds) 1989, *Art and Society: Readings in the Sociology of the Arts*, State University of New York Press, Albany

Foucault, Michel 1991, 'Governmentality', in *The Foucault Effect: Studies in Governmentality*, eds Graham Burchell, Colin Gordon and Peter Miller, University of Chicago Press, Chicago, pp. 87–104

——1997, *Ethics: Essential Works of Foucault 1954–1984, Volume 1*, ed. Paul Rabinow, Penguin, London

Fowler, Bridget 1997, *Pierre Bourdieu and Cultural Theory: Critical Investigations*, Sage, London

Frow, John 1995, *Cultural Studies and Cultural Value*, Clarendon Press, Oxford

Grenfell, Michael and David James, with Philip Hodkinson, Diane Reay and Derek Robbins 1998, *Bourdieu and Education: Acts of Practical Theory*, Falmer Press, London

Harker, R., C. Mahar and C. Wilkes 1990, *An Introduction to the Work of Pierre Bourdieu*, Macmillan, London

Hawkes, Terence 1977, *Structuralism and Semiotics*, Methuen, London

Jenkins, Richard 1992, *Pierre Bourdieu*, Routledge, London and New York

Kauppi, Niilo 2000, *The Politics of Embodiment: Habit, Power and Pierre Bourdieu's Theory*, Peter Lang Publishing, New York

Laclau, Ernesto and Chantal Mouffe 1990, *Hegemony and Socialist Strategy*, Verso, London

Lane, Jeremy 2000, *Pierre Bourdieu: A Critical Introduction*, Pluto Press, London

Nash, Roy 1999, 'Bourdieu, "habitus", and educational research: is it all worth the candle?' *British Journal of Sociology of Education*, vol. 20, no. 2, June, pp. 175–87

Nietzsche, Friedrich 1966, *Beyond Good and Evil*, trans. W. Kaufmann, Vintage Books, New York

——1969, *On the Genealogy of Morals*, trans. W. Kaufmann and R.J. Hollingdale, Vintage Books, New York

Panofsky, Erwin 1955, *Meaning in the Visual Arts: Papers in and on Art History*, Overlook Press, Woodstock NY

Robbins, Derek 1991, *The Work of Pierre Bourdieu: Recognizing Society*, Open University Press, Milton Keynes

Schirato, Tony and Susan Yell 2000, *Communication and Cultural Literacy: An Introduction*, 2nd edn, Sage, London

Shusterman, Richard (ed) 1999, *Bourdieu: A Critical Reader*, Blackwell, Oxford

Simmel, Georg 1998, 'On the sociology of the family' *Theory, Culture and Society*, 15/3–4, pp. 283–93

Staniszewski, Mary Anne 1995, *Believing is Seeing: Creating the Culture of Art*, Penguin, Harmondsworth

Swartz, David 1997, *Culture and Power: The Sociology of Pierre Bourdieu*, University of Chicago Press, Chicago

Index